LONDON

GUIDE IN COLOUR

(Cover) Westminster Bridge and The Houses of Parliament.
Westminster Bridge and Big Ben.

CONTENTS

SHORT BREAKS
IN LONDON

Visitors with only a limited amount of time at their disposal should try to take in as many of the following "essential" sights as possible. Public transport facilities are given below and opening times may be found on p. 186. It is worth picking up a bus and underground map from a London Transport or London Tourist Board Information Centre.

Westminster Abbey (see First Itinerary)
Underground station: Westminster.
Buses: 3, 11, 12, 24, 29, 53, 77, 77A, 88, 109, 159, 170, 184.
London's most magnificent Gothic church, scene of the coronation of English sovereigns since 1066, containing monuments to many great figures in British history. Of particular interest are Poets' Corner, around Chaucer's tomb, the sumptuous Royal Tombs, the Coronation Chair with the Stone of Scone and Henry VII's Chapel, one of the supreme glories of late Perpendicular architecture.

The National Gallery (see Second Itinerary)
Underground station: Charing Cross, Leicester Square.
Buses: 1, 3, 6, 9, 11, 12, 13, 15, 15B, 22B, 24, 29, 53, 77, 77A, 88, 109, 159, 170, 176, 184, 196.
On the north side of Trafalgar Square stands one of the world's greatest art galleries, representing all schools of Western painting from the Italian Primitives to the early 20th century. Its collections include such masterpieces as Leonardo da Vinci's Virgin and Child with St. Anne cartoon, Piero della Francesca's Baptism of Christ, Van Eyck's Arnolfini Marriage, Van Dyck's Equestrian Portrait of Charles I and the Rokeby Venus by Velasquez.

Buckingham Palace (see Third Itinerary)
Underground station: Victoria, St. James's Park, Green Park.
Buses: 2, 2B, 11, 14, 16, 19, 22, 24, 25, 29, 30, 36, 36B, 38, 52, 52A, 73, 74, 76, 82, 135, 137, 185, 507.
The London residence of the sovereign since the reign of Queen Victoria. The colourful ceremony of Changing the Guard takes place in the forecourt at 11.30 (daily in summer, alternate days in winter, telephone London Tourist Board on 071-730 3488 to check). Nearby St. James's Park is also worth a visit.

The Tower of London (see Ninth Itinerary)
Underground station: Tower Hill.
Buses: 15, 25, 42, 78, 100, 510.
Since the time of William the Conqueror the Tower has served as a fortress, royal residence, treasury, mint, menagerie and prison. Watched over by the Beefeaters, or Yeomen Warders, the complex of walls, towers and other buildings are grouped around the original nucleus of the White Tower, built by William I. Of particular note are the collections of arms and armour, the Crown Jewels, the Chapel of St. John (the oldest in London), Traitors' Gate and the executioner's block.

The British Museum (see Seventh Itinerary)
Underground station: Tottenham Court Road, Goodge

Parliament Square.
Westminster Bridge.

Street, Russell Square.

Buses: 7, 8, 10, 14, 19, 22B, 24, 25, 29, 38, 55, 68, 73, 77A, 134, 176, 188, 503.

Probably the most comprehensive museum in the world, representing man's most important cultural achievements since prehistoric times, from the monumental sculptures of ancient Egypt to the perfection of Classical Greek art; from the Rosetta Stone to exquisite illuminated manuscripts; from Assyrian reliefs to superb Medieval craftmanship.

St. Paul's Cathedral (see Ninth Itinerary)

Underground station: St. Paul's.

Buses: 4, 6, 8, 9, 11, 15, 17, 25, 76, 141, 501, 502, 513.

The present building is the masterpiece of Sir Christopher Wren, who made it the focal point of his network of City churches built after the Great Fire of 1666. The majestic dome is one of London's best-known landmarks and its galleries afford superb views over the City. The sumptuous interior contains the monuments and tombs of many famous figures, including Wren himself, Wellington, Nelson and John Donne. The Whispering Gallery is famous for its curious sound effects.

The Victoria and Albert Museum (see Fifth Itinerary)

Underground station: South Kensington.

Buses: 14, 30, 45, 49, 74, 503, C1.

Occupying a 12-acre site, the "V & A" is a repository for some of the finest examples of the applied and decorative arts of all kinds from all over the world. It houses huge collections of furniture, jewellery, statuary, costumes, textiles, musical instruments, silverware and metalwork. It also houses the Raphael Cartoons for tapestries made for Pope Leo X and the largest public collection of the works of John Constable.

The Tate Galley (see First Itinerary)

Underground station: Pimlico.

Buses: 2, 2B, 3, 36, 36B, 77A, 88, 185, 507.

The gallery houses the national collection of British

painting from the Renaissance to the present, with an excellent selection of contemporary works as well as splendid 18th century paintings by Reynolds, Gainsborough and Constable. Foreign modern art is also well represented and regular temporary exhibitions are held. The displays are regularly rotated, as not all the collection can be seen at one time.

The Courtauld Institute Galleries (see Eighth Itinerary)
Underground stations: Temple, Covent Garden, Aldwych (rush hour only).
Buses: 1, 4, 6, 9, 11, 13, 15, 68, 77, 168, 170, 171, 176, 188, 196, 501, 502, 505, 513.
Housed in the restored north wing of Somerset House, the collection is best known for its superb array of Impressionist and Post-Impressionist paintings, including Manet's Bar at the Folies-Bergère and Renoir's La Loge. There are also some fine Old Masters, including works by Cranach, Rubens and Tiepolo.

The Wallace Collection, (see Sixth Itinerary)
Underground station: Baker Street, Bond Street.
Buses: 2, 2B, 6, 7, 8, 10, 12, 13, 15, 16A, 30, 73, 74, 88, 113, 135, 137, 503.
A private collection housed in the elegant town house of the Marquesses of Hertford. It is particularly rich in 18th century French paintings, porcelain and furniture, but also contains fine displays of arms and armour. Its most famous painting is Hals' Laughing Cavalier.

Sir John Soane's Museum (see Eighth Itinerary)
Underground station: Holborn.
Buses: 1, 4, 7, 8, 25, 38, 55, 68, 77A, 170, 171, 188, 196, 501, 505.
The collections of the connoisseur and architect of the Bank of England are displayed in the house he built for himself. They reflect his own taste and personality and include many antiquities and fine paintings, including the sarcophagus of Seti I and Hogarth's Rake's Progress and Election series of paintings.

HISTORICAL INTRODUCTION

The history of London is naturally inextricably linked with the history of the country itself, as the brief background given here shows.

The name London most probably derives from the Celtic Llyn (a lake) and Dun (a fort or strong place), although the site was not important during the Celtic period. The settlement grew rapidly in Roman times between the incursions of Julius Ceasar in 54 B.C. and the actual conquest of Britain which began under the Emperor Claudius in 43 A.D.

During the Roman occupation Londinium, as it was then known, was not important in a political sense, but flourished as the major port of the island province as its position on the Thames estuary was ideal for shipping to and from the Continent. All the famous Roman roads in Britain converged upon London from the north and south and mileage was calculated from a stone in the Forum of Agricola, now known as the London stone, which can be seen today in the wall of the Bank of China in Cannon Street. The course of the fortified wall built around Londinium can still be traced and fragments of it can be seen. It marked the boundaries of the city in Medieval times and roughly corresponds to the square mile of the City as we know it today. The present Tower of London at Tower Hill is built on the site of a Roman fort and the position of the Roman gates of the city are recorded in modern names such as Aldgate, Aldersgate and Ludgate.

In 61 A.D., the city was attacked and devastated by Boadicea, queen of the northern Iceni tribe, who defeated the renowned Tenth Legion, but was then herself defeated by a contingent led by Suetonius Paulinus. After this abortive threat to its sovereignty, Roman rule continued until early in the 5th century when Roman forces were withdrawn from Britain to cope with troubles elsewhere in the Empire.

It was only much later, after invading Saxons settled on the site of the Roman city that London became a capital, chosen as such by the powerful Saxon king, Alfred the Great who reigned from 871-899 and set about repairing the city's defences. The reign of Edward the Confessor (1042-66) saw the first Norman influences in Britain. He built Westminster Abbey, and most important for the future development of the city, established his own royal residence on nearby Thorney Island, outside the city walls, and granted certain rights to the citizens within. The Battle of Hastings in 1066 marked the last successful invasion of Britain. William, Duke of Normandy, took the British throne as William I, initiating a strong, centralized rule with London at its heart. He built the White Tower, nucleus of the Tower of London in 1087 and granted a city charter laying down the rights of its citizens. His son, William Rufus, built Westminster Palace and Westminster Hall which was to remain the seat of the Palace of Justice until 1882. The first mayor of the city, Henry Fitz Aylwin, was elected in 1191, during the reign of Richard I, the Lionheart.

Throughout the Norman and Plantagenet eras, the legal and parliamentary systems of the country were slowly evolving. William I separated the secular from the ecclesiastical courts and gave himself the right to appoint British prelates. During the reign of Henry I the Court of the Exchequer was settled at Westminster while the Curia Regis continued to follow the king around the country. Under Henry II, further law reforms were instigated and a bench of royal judges established to administer the Common Law.

In 1215 the increasingly powerful barons managed to force King John to sign the Magna Carta which stipulated *inter alia* that no *"extraordinary scutage or aid shall be imposed on our kingdom unless by common council of our kingdom"*, and *"in like manner it shall be done concerning aid from the city of London"*. In 1265 two worthy citizens and two knights from each borough and shire (county) were summoned to Parliament in London.

The 14th century was a turbulent period. In 1337 the long and costly Hundred Years War against France began; the Black Death of 1348 claimed the lives of over a quarter of the British people; in 1381 the grievances of the lower classes exploded into the "Peasants' Revolt". The injustices suffered by this class were brought to a head by the poll tax levied as yet another source of funding the war with France. Insurgents were admitted into the city of London by sympathisers where they held the young King Richard II prisoner in the Tower for several days. At Smithfield, a meeting with the king was arranged, but the Mayor of London treacherously killed the peasant leader, Wat Tyler. Despite, or perhaps in

Westminster Bridge and the Houses of Parliament, at night

some ways, because of these troubles, there was at this time an enormous feeling of national pride and a tremendous advance in the English language as seen, for example, in the writings of Chaucer.

England, however, was still not free from strife as the baronial Wars of the Roses between the rival houses of

York and Lancaster followed almost immediately after the Hundred Years War. It ended with the defeat of the Lancastrian Richard III, "Crookback", at Bosworth Fields in 1485 by the Welsh Henry Tudor who then reigned as Henry VII. This wise and cautious king was succeeded by a man of remarkably different character, the flamboyant Henry VIII, of the six wives – "*divorced, beheaded, died, divorced, beheaded, survived*". Like his father, however, Henry VIII enjoyed the continuing support of Parliament; the Act of Supremacy in 1534, making the crown the spiritual head of the nation, was discussed and approved by both houses. This led to the decisive breach with the papacy and the resulting Dissolution of the Monasteries gave Henry a vast and much-needed revenue since, in London alone, a quarter of all property was church-owned.

The Elizabethan period (1558-1603) is often considered to be a golden age in British history. Elizabeth I, known equally as "Good Queen Bess", a "Faerie Queene" and a "mere woman" was a cultivated person who had benefited from a brilliant European Renaissance education and harboured a private desire "to teach still peace to grow". Amongst her successes was Drake's defeat to the famed Spanish Armada which had threatened her reign; but an unhappy time followed when she was forced to order the execution of her cousin, Mary Queen of Scots in order to quell rumours of royal plots and restore peace and order to the country. She managed, with the help of Sir Thomas Gresham and the establishment of the Royal Exchange, to improve somewhat the appalling financial system left by her father. She also took a great interest in the Royal Navy which he had founded. This was a time of maritime adventure and the exploits of Drake, Hawkins, Raleigh and the like were followed with great excitement. There was much overseas exploration, settlement and trade and in 1600 the East India Company charter was granted. It was also the period of the English Renaissance, celebrated by the works of Shakespeare and other writers and the revolution in architecture led by Inigo Jones and based on Italian models, especially the work of Andrea Palladio.

By contrast, the accession to the English throne of James VI of Scotland, Mary Queen of Scots' son, saw the beginning of the unhappy Stuart dynasty. Parliament was neglected – summoned only as a source of finance – and there were religious problems, in particular the promulgation of the theory of Divine Right which was detrimental to the relationship between crown and people. These and other difficulties culminated in civil war and the execution of Charles I on January 30th 1649, followed by the establishment of the short-lived Puritan Republic under Oliver Cromwell.

When the Stuart line was restored, with Charles II taking the throne in 1660, the British responded with an exuberant display of fashion, theatre, pleasure-seeking and extravagance. They enjoyed royal patronage of the arts and sciences, in particular of Sir Isaac Newton and the Royal Society which was granted its Royal Charter in 1662. Unfortunately, events soon took another downturn when in 1665 the Great Plague was responsible for the deaths of 100,000 Londoners and the following year perhaps London's greatest disaster occurred. The Great Fire, thought to have started in Pudding Lane, raged for three days, destroying in its wake some 13,000 houses, the Royal Exchange, St. Paul's Cathedral, 86 churches and most of the guildhalls, over an area of almost 400 acres; the Tower of London had a lucky escape. One positive effect of the fire was to rid the Medieval city of its accumulated filth. The architect, Sir Christopher Wren, lost no time in drawing up plans giving the entire city a monumental Baroque aspect. Many of these plans were never realized as people immediately began rebuilding for themselves, but his achievement of more than 50 churches, including St. Paul's Cathedral, was quite remarkable.

The Georgian era was one of enormous expansion when London was considered the premier city of the Western world, with fashions set by the Prince Regent and Beau Brummel, the stately architecture and planning of Nash and the elegant coffee houses and clubs. The Bank of England was established in 1694, a year after the National Debt.

By the time of George III's death the city's outskirts stretched as far as Hammersmith, Deptford, Highgate and Paddington, but it was during the extremely prosperous Victorian era that London became the metropolis it is today Britain's wealth and prestige at the height of her Imperial power is expressed in the public buildings erected at that time, such as the Houses of Parliament, and in the development of industry and public transport.

The Second World War had a devastating effect, almost equal to that of the Great Fire, destroying large areas of the city. New buildings continue to change the face of London, but it remains a centre for fashion, culture and artistic achievement.

FIRST ITINERARY

WESTMINSTER BRIDGE - HOUSES OF PARLIAMENT - ST MARGARET'S CHURCH - PARLIAMENT SQUARE - WESTMINSTER ABBEY - TATE GALLERY

Westminster was created when Edward the Confessor moved his residence here and built his abbey church on what was then Thorney Island. The Palace of Westminster remained the sovereign's principal residence until Henry VIII took over Cardinal Wolsey's palace, York Place, renaming it Whitehall.

Westminster Bridge, completed in 1862 to designs by Thomas Page, affords an excellent view upriver of the grandiose complex of the **Houses of Parliament** and the

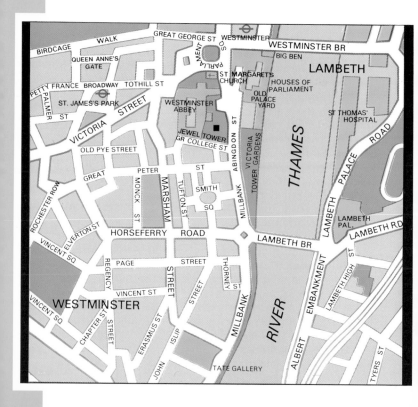

wide sweep of the Thames towards the City. On this site, though not on this actual bridge, Wordsworth proclaimed that "Earth has not anything to show more fair". In 1834 fire destroyed most of the original Palace of Westminster, though Westminster Hall and the crypt and cloisters of St. Stephen's Chapel survived to be incorporated into the present Houses of Parliament, designed in late-Gothic style by Sir Charles Barry with the help of Augustus Pugin. The site covers eight acres, with eleven courtyards, two miles of passages and an 872ft. facade overlooking the Thames. Building began in 1840 and it was completed in 1888.

On the corner next to Westminster Bridge stands St. Stephen's Tower which houses the famous 13.5 ton bell, "Big Ben", which chimes the hours. It is named after Sir Benjamin Hall, who was Commissioner of Works when it was hung. Each clock face is 23ft. in diameter and the figures are 2ft. high. A light at the top of the tower at night indicates that Parliament is sitting.

New Palace Yard on the left leads past Westminster Hall and Thornycroft's statue of Oliver Cromwell (1899) to Old Palace Yard, where the Royal Entrance is situated under Victoria Tower. To the left is Marochetti's statue of Richard I (1860). The Royal Staircase leads up through the Norman Porch to the Queen's Robing Room, lined in rich wood panelling and decorated with frescoes on the legend of King Arthur. At the State Opening of Parliament the sovereign now passes along the Royal Gallery, through the Prince's Chamber, with a white marble statue of Queen Victoria, into the House of Lords. Here Pugin's sumptuous decoration and frescoes by Maclise, Cope, Dyce and Horsley provide a dramatic backdrop for more than 1000 lords who sit on red benches before the Throne, from where the sovereign declares the Opening of Parliament. Separated from the Throne by a gilt rail is the Lord Chancellor's seat, the Woolsack, a plain seat stuffed with wool – this is a tradition dating back to the reign of Edward III, when the wool trade was so important to the country's economy. At the opposite end of the House members of the House of Commons gather at the Bar to hear the sovereign speak, and above this the Galleries provide seating for distinguished visitors and "strangers" (members of the public).

Above the north and south doors of the Peers' Lobby are the arms of the six Royal dynasties, Saxon, Norman, Plantagenet, Tudor, Stuart and Hanoverian and in the

HOUSES OF PARLIAMENT

Peers' Corridor are frescoes of the Stuart and Commonwealth periods by Cope. The octagonal Central Lobby
leads on through the Commons' Corridor and the Commons' Lobby, graced by the Churchill Arch, into the
House of Commons, whose decoration is much more
severe than that of the House of Lords. It suffered

Aerial View of the Houses of Parliament.

serious damage during World War II and was rebuilt by Sir Giles Gilbert Scott and reopened in 1950. The Speaker's Chair faces the chamber at the north end, with the government benches ranged on his right and the opposition benches on his left. Above are the press and public galleries.

Also leading off the Central Lobby is St. Stephen's Hall, on the site of the original St. Stephen's Chapel, which was the meeting-place of the House of Commons for nearly three centuries. From here St. Stephen's Porch

Statue of Boadicea

gives access to Westminster Hall, originally constructed in 1097 for William II and rebuilt in 1397 by Henry Yevele for Richard II. It boasts a splendid oak hammer-beam roof. From 1224 to 1882 the Hall served as England's chief law courts and many momentous historic events have taken place here, including the trial of Charles I in 1649 and the trials of Sir Thomas More, Sir Thomas Wyatt and Guy Fawkes. In 1653 Oliver Cromwell took the oath here as Lord Protector, but in 1661 his head was set on a pole on the roof of the Hall. In the south-east corner steps lead down to St. Stephen's Crypt which formed part of the original chapel built by Edward I.

Opposite the Houses of Parliament is **St. Margaret's Church**, which serves as the parish church of the House of Commons. The present building, by Robert Stowell, dates from 1485-1523, but was refaced in the 18th century. The magnificent East Window, representing the Crucifixion, is 16th century Dutch glass, but was not installed until 1758. It was originally intended to celebrate the betrothal of Catherine of Aragon to Prince Arthur, elder brother of Henry VIII, but before it arrived Henry had become king and married her himself. Samuel Pepys, John Milton and Winston Churchill were all married in the church.

The House of Lords.

Big Ben.

Parliament Square was laid out in 1868 by Sir Charles Barry, architect of the Houses of Parliament. It is now little more than a busy traffic roundabout, but round its borders are a number of statues to statesmen, the most striking being that of Sir Winston Churchill by Ivor

Parliament Square with the Houses of Parliament.

Roberts-Jones (1973).
Towering above St. Margaret's Church is **Westminster Abbey**, or, to give it its correct name, the Collegiate Church of St. Peter. According to tradition the first church on the site was built by King Sebert and conse-

crated in 616 by Mellitus, the first Bishop of London. By 750 there was a Benedictine abbey here, but in 1065 a new abbey was consecrated by Edward the Confessor. Later Henry III decided to rebuild the church to house the shrine of St. Edward, and it is basically this church, completed in 1269, with a few later additions, that we see before us. The main additions to the building are Henry VII's Chapel and the western towers, which were added in 1789.

William the Conqueror was crowned in the Abbey on Christmas Day 1066, and since then all English sovereigns, with the exception of Edward V and Edward VIII, have been crowned here, and most were buried here until the early 19th century. Also buried or commemorated here are many eminent (and some not so eminent) people, and there are many splendid monuments.

Entry to the Abbey is through the West Door and from here you can appreciate the Gothic splendour of the interior. At 102ft. this is the highest nave in England. Just inside the entrance is a memorial to Sir Winston

Westminster Abbey. The Façade

Churchill, and beyond that the Tomb of the Unknown Warrior, a simple slab of black Belgian marble commemorating the fallen in the First World War. Before moving on, note, on a pillar, the portrait of Richard II, the oldest portrait of an English sovereign.

Now pass down the North Choir Aisle, or Musicians' Aisle, which contains memorials to Purcell, Elgar and

Aerial view of Westminster Bridge

Britten. This leads to the North Transept, or Statesmen's Aisle, with many impressive monuments to 19th century politicians. Under the crossing is the Sanctuary, the spot where coronations take place. The floor in front of the 19th century altar is usually covered to protect a beautiful Cosmati pavement of 1268. On the north side of the Sanctuary are three fine medieval tombs and on the south side are the 14th century sedilia and the tomb of Anne of Cleves, Henry VIII's fourth wife.

Continuing down the North Ambulatory you pass the Chapels of St. John the Baptist and of St. Paul. Before you reach Henry VII's Chapel, visit the north aisle of the chapel which contains the impressive tomb of Elizabeth I (ironically her sister, Mary I, is buried in the same tomb). Beyond are the touching tombs of two daughters of James I who died in infancy and a small sarcophagus containing bones supposedly of the two sons of Edward IV killed in the Tower.

Westminster Abbey, Interior

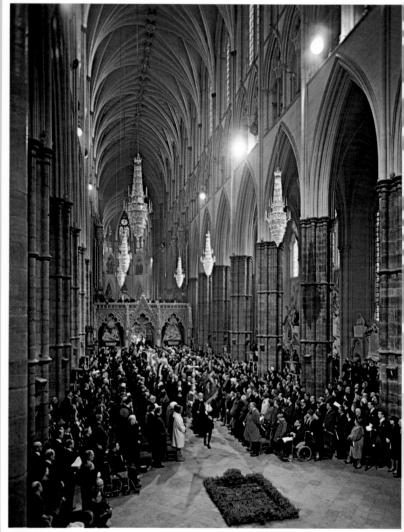

Next comes Henry VII's Chapel, named after its founder. Built 1503-19, it is the finest example of late Perpendicular architecture in England, culminating in the graceful tracery of the fan vaulting. Along both sides are the stalls of the Knights of the Bath with their banners hanging above them. Note the carved misericords on the undersides of the seats. The fine tomb behind the altar is of Henry VII and his wife, by Torrigiani. James I is buried in the same tomb, and Edward VI and George II are buried elsewhere in the chapel.

A bridge takes you past the tomb of Henry V into the heart of the Abbey, the Chapel of St. Edward the Confessor. In the centre is the shrine itself, still retaining a few traces of its original rich mosaic decoration. Around the sides of the chapel are splendid tombs to Henry III, builder of the Abbey, and to Edward I, his queen, Eleanor of Castille, Richard II and his queen, Anne of Bohemia and Edward III and his queen, Philippa of Hainault. Against the 15th century screen is the Coronation Chair, made for Edward I. Underneath it is the Stone of Scone, used for the coronations of the kings of Scotland and taken by Edward I in 1297.

Re-crossing the bridge you reach the south aisle of Henry VII's Chapel, which contains the tomb of Mary, Queen of Scots, the last royal tomb put up in the Abbey.

Westminster Abbey, Interior: the Choir

Westminster Abbey: the Coronation Chair enclosing the Stone of Scone

The tomb of Margaret Beaumont, Countess of Richmond has another fine effigy by Torrigiani, and in a vault at the end are buried Charles II, William III, Mary II and Queen Anne.

Returning to the Ambulatory you now pass the Chapels of St. Nicholas and St. Edmund, the latter containing two fine monumental brasses. This leads you to the South Transept, better known as Poets' Corner. Here you can admire the many tombs and memorials to writers, musicians and actors, including Chaucer, Shakespeare, Milton and Handel. The two 13th century wall paintings were uncovered in 1936. Look out for the grave of Thomas Parr who died in 1635 aged 152! The door at the end of the South Choir Aisle leads into the Cloisters, on the east side of which are the Chapter

Westminster Abbey: Chapel of Henry VII

House, Chamber of the Pyx and the Museum. The 13th century Chapter House was where Parliament met from 1352 to 1547. There is a fine 13th century pavement and the walls still retain traces of 14th century paintings. The Chamber of the Pyx is part of the original 11th century church and was once the royal treasury. The Museum was once the undercroft of the dormitory of the original church. It houses a number of wax funeral effigies, among them Charles II dressed in his garter robes. There are also wooden effigies of Edward III and Henry VII, as well as a wax figure of Lord Nelson. Among other interesting items are the coronation chair made for Mary II and copies of the Coronation regalia used for rehearsals. Leaving the Abbey through Dean's Yard, return to Parliament Square and turn right down Abingdon Street.

TATE GALLERY

On the right is the **Jewel Tower**, built for Edward III as a private treasury and now a museum. In Victoria Tower Gardens opposite is a copy of Rodin's sculpture the Burghers of Calais. Continue down Millbank and, looking down Dean Stanley Street you will see, in Smith Square, the unusual baroque church of St. John the Evangelist, now a concert hall. Just before you reach Lambeth Bridge there is a fine view across the Thames of Lambeth Palace, the London residence of the Archbishop of Canterbury.

A little way further down Millbank you will come to the

The Tate Gallery, Exterior

Tate Gallery, which houses an extensive collection of British painting from Tudor times and modern art and sculpture from Britain and abroad. It began with a gift of 65 paintings from Sir Henry Tate, the sugar magnate. He also commissioned the building, which opened in 1897. It has been extended on a number of occasions, most recently with the addition of the Clore Gallery in 1987. The collection has recently been rearranged in chronological sequence, but, owing to the size of the collection, it cannot all be shown at the same time and many rooms will be changed on a regular basis. A free plan of the gallery is available at the information desk showing the current displays.

The earliest painting on display is John Bettes' Man in a

Tate Gallery, William Blake: Elohim creating Adam

Black Cap of 1545. Other early paintings include a portrait of Elizabeth I by Nicholas Hilliard and portraits by Lely and Kneller. There are several pictures by Hogarth including the famous self-portrait, Portrait of the Painter and his Pug. The 18th century is represented by Reynolds, Stubbs and Gainsborough, including the latter's

Tate Gallery. J.M.W. Turner, Storm at Sea.

portrait of Giovanna Baccelli. There is a fine collection
of paintings by Constable, including Flatford Mill, and
other 19th century artists include Blake, Fuseli, Landseer and Richard Dadd. The extensive Turner collection
is now housed in the Clore Gallery; it covers all periods
of his output, from an early self-portrait to several
impressive late works, including the famous Snow
Storm. There is a large collection of works by the Pre-
Raphaelites including paintings by Millais, Holman
Hunt and Rossetti. The collection of Impressionist
paintings includes works by Monet, Gauguin, Sickert,

Tate Gallery, Roy Lichtenstein: Whaam!

Whistler and Sargent. The modern collection takes up more than half the gallery and includes examples of all the major schools. As well as an ever-changing display of contemporary works, there are paintings by Picasso, Léger, Dalí, Bacon and Pollock as well as sculpture by Rodin, Giacometti and Henry Moore.

The restaurant in the basement enjoys an excellent reputation, and is also notable for a fine mural by Rex Whistler.

A number of buses will take you back to Westminster and Pimlico Underground station is only a short walk away.

Westminster Abbey by Night

SECOND ITINERARY

TRAFALGAR SQUARE - ST. MARTIN-IN-THE-FIELDS - NATIONAL GALLERY - NATIONAL PORTRAIT GALLERY - WHITEHALL - CABINET WAR ROOMS

Trafalgar Square, famous for its pigeons, demonstrations and New Year revelries, was laid out by Sir Charles Barry in 1829-41 on the site of the Royal Mews. Its name commemorates the great naval battle of 1805 when the French fleet was defeated by the English under Admiral Lord Nelson, whose monument dominates the square. The 170ft. monument, known as Nelson's Column, was designed by William Railton and the 16ft. statue of Nelson by E.H. Baily was erected in 1843. The four bronze reliefs at the base of the column illustrate naval battles and were cast from captured French cannon. The bronze lions by Landseer were cast by Marochetti and erected in 1867. The two fountains designed by Lutyens

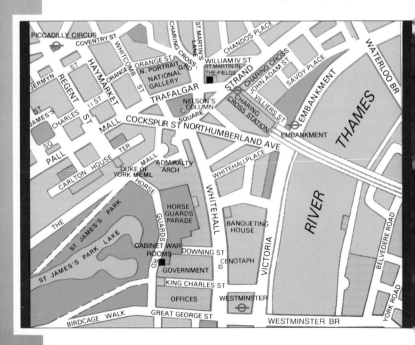

Trafalgar Square

were added in 1939. Every Christmas a fir tree is donated by the people of Norway and set up in the square.

At the north-east corner of the square stands the church of **St. Martin-in-the-Fields**. It was built by James Gibbs in 1722-24, though there were two former churches on the site. The elegant interior contains a 17th century font from the previous church and an ornate ceiling by Artari and Bagutti. The church holds regular lunchtime concerts and in the crypt are a restaurant, bookshop and the London Brass Rubbing Centre.

Spanning the whole of the north side of the square is the **National Gallery** which houses one of the world's great art collections. It began in 1824 with the purchase by the government of 38 paintings belonging to the late John Julius Angerstein, a rich merchant. As the collection grew more space was needed, and in 1838 it moved to the present building, the work of William Wilkins. Over the

NATIONAL GALLERY

years the building has been extended on a number of occasions, and the latest addition, the Sainsbury Wing, is due to open in 1991. Many improvements are currently being carried out. Rooms are being restored, improved lighting and air-conditioning are being installed, and much of the collection is being rehung. A free floor-plan is available to help you find your way around the gallery, and what follows is only a summary of some of the highlights of the collection.

Trafalgar Square with the National Gallery to the left and the Church of St. Martin-in-the-Fields to the right

ITALIAN PAINTING

The early Sienese artist, Duccio, is represented by a beautiful triptych, The Virgin and Child with Saints. Fra Angelico's Christ Glorified in the Court of Heaven is filled with angels playing musical instruments. Uccello's interest in perspective can be seen in his vivid Battle of San Romano. There are three fine paintings by Botticelli, including Venus and Mars, with its playful satyrs, and Mystic Nativity, his only signed work. The Baptism of Christ and the Nativity are two of Piero della Francesca's greatest works, with their delicate colours and strong composition. Hanging side by side are two very different interpretations of the Agony in the Garden, by Mantegna and his brother-in-law, Bellini. The famous

National Gallery, Rembrandt van Rijn: Self-portrait at 63

Leonardo da Vinci cartoon of The Virgin and Child with Saints Anne and John the Baptist can be seen in a special room of its own. Also on display is his haunting Virgin of the Rocks. Even though unfinished, Michelangelo's Entombment is a powerful composition. There are several works by Raphael including the Ansidei Madonna and the portrait of Pope Julius II. Of several works by Titian, perhaps the most striking is the colourful Bacchus and Ariadne. Equally striking is the simple realism of Caravaggio's The Supper at Emmaus. The Stonemason's Yard is one of Canaletto's more unusual and atmospheric views of Venice.

National Gallery, Anthony Van Dyck: Equestrian portrait of Charles I

EARLY NEDERLANDISH PAINTING

Justly famous is Van Eyck's Marriage of Giovanni Arnolfini, with its wealth of detail. Also worthy of note are Rogier van der Weyden's Pietà, Memlinc's Donne Triptych and Hieronymus Bosch's Christ Mocked.

GERMAN PAINTING

The small German collection includes Dürer's portrait of his father, Cranach's delightful Cupid Complaining to

Venus and Holbein's extraordinary The Ambassadors, with a distorted skull in the foreground.

FLEMISH PAINTING
There are several works by Rubens, notably the Judgement of Paris and the portrait of Susanna Lunden, known as Le Chapeau de Paille. Also note Van Dyck's Equestrian Portrait of Charles I.

DUTCH PAINTING
Dutch art of the 16th and 17th centuries is well represented, with landscapes by, among others, Ruisdael and Cuyp. Avercamp's Winter Scene with Skaters is particularly charming, and Hobbema's The Avenue,

National Gallery, Diego Velasquez: The Toilet of Venus (the "Rokeby Venus")

Middelharnis is a striking composition. Among many domestic scenes, Vermeer's A Young Woman Standing at a Virginal is notable. There are a number of fine works by Rembrandt, including a Self-Portrait aged Sixty-Three, A Woman Bathing in a Stream and the dramatic Belshazzar's Feast.

SPANISH PAINTING
There are two works by El Greco, including Agony in the Garden, a Self-Portrait by Murillo, Velazquez' Portrait of Philip IV and his famous Toilet of Venus ("The

Rokeby Venus"). There are also two fine portraits by Goya, of Doña Isabel de Porcel and the Duke of Wellington.

BRITISH PAINTING

The six satirical scenes of Hogarth's Marriage à la Mode are worthy of close study, and there are several good portraits by Reynolds and Gainsborough, notably the latter's The Morning Walk and Mr and Mrs Andrews. Constable's The Haywain and Turner's The "Fighting Téméraire" are possibly the best known of all British paintings.

FRENCH PAINTING

One of the gems of the whole collection is the Wilton Diptych, an exquisite late 14th century work showing Richard II being presented to the Virgin and Child. From the 17th century there are landscapes and classical scenes by Claude (The Embarkation of the Queen of Sheba) and Poussin (The Adoration of the Golden Calf). From the 19th century there are works by Delacroix, Ingres and Corot. There is a good collection of Impressionist paintings, including Monet's atmospheric Gare St-Lazare, Renoir's Les Parapluies, Degas' stunning La La at the Cirque Fernando and Van Gogh's Sunflowers. Other highlights include Seurat's Bathers at Asnières, Rousseau's Tropical Storm with a Tiger and Cezanne's Les Grandes Baigneuses.

THE BERGGRUEN COLLECTION

A superb group of late 19th and 20th century art from the collection of Heinz Berggruen is currently on extended loan to the gallery. It includes works by Braque, Mirò, Cezanne, Van Gogh and Seurat as well as no less than forty by Picasso, spanning most of his career.

The **National Portrait Gallery** is situated behind the National Gallery, with its entrance in St. Martin's Place. It was founded in 1856 and contains a vast collection of portraits of famous British men and women. Although the emphasis is on the people, there are many fine works of art and many great artists are represented. The collection is arranged chronologically, starting at the top of the building, and the rooms are furnished so as to give a sense of period. Only a quarter of the collection can be displayed at any one time, and the gallery is currently being expanded to allow for improved displays, particularly of the 20th century portraits.

Take the lift to the second floor and walk down to the mezzanine, where you will find the earliest portraits, of the Tudor period. There is a portrait of Henry VII by Sittow and a Holbein cartoon of Henry VIII and Henry VII, as well as a strange, distorted portrait of Edward VI which has to be viewed from the side to be seen in perspective. There are three impressive likenesses of Elizabeth I and a number of miniatures, among them Drake and Raleigh by Hilliard. The "Chandos portrait" of Shakespeare is the only known contemporary likeness. Moving on into the Stuart rooms, as well as all the monarchs, there are portraits of Cromwell, Milton, Pepys and Ben Jonson. Note Van Dyck's splendid painting of Venetia Stanley, Lady Digby and portraits of Nell Gwyn and the Duchess of Portsmouth, two of Charles II's mistresses. There are several fine portraits by Kneller, including one of Sir Christopher Wren. In the Georgian section there are portraits by Reynolds, Gainsborough and Hogarth, including self-portraits. The many subjects include Swift, Handel, Johnson and Boswell (both by Reynolds). Side by side are portraits of Lord Nelson (by Beechey) and Lady Hamilton (by Romney). Romantic writers include Keats, Byron, Shelley and Wordsworth.

The Victorian period is extensively covered, including, as well as portraits of Queen Victoria and Prince Albert, paintings, prints and photographs of eminent people from all walks of life, writers, musicians, engineers and politicians. Writers include Tennyson, Hardy, Dickens (by Maclise) and the Bronte Sisters in the famous group portrait by their brother, Branwell. Political rivals Gladstone and Disraeli hang side by side, both portrayed by Millais, and there is a delightful picture of Ellen Terry as a child. The 20th century, now newly displayed, includes portraits of the current royal family, some controversial, and a wide range of famous personalities, politicians, musicians, writers and film stars.

Returning to Trafalgar Square, you will see, over to the right, **Admiralty Arch**, which stands at the entrance to the Mall, which leads down to Buckingham Palace. It was designed by Sir Aston Webb as a memorial to Queen Victoria. The central gate is usually closed as only the sovereign may pass through it. On the south side of the square stands the equestrian statue of Charles I by Le

Sueur. It stands on the site of the original Charing Cross and a bronze plaque in the pavement marks the official centre of London. The statue was sold for scrap after the Civil War, but at the Restoration was found to be intact and erected here in 1675.

N° 10, Downing Street.

2

Stretching south from Trafalgar Square is **Whitehall**, which contains many government offices. On the left are Great Scotland Yard, home of the Metropolitan Police until the end of the 19th century, and the Ministry of Defence. On the right are the Admiralty and, further down, **Horse Guards**, designed by William Kent. The mounted guard by the Household Cavalry is relieved every hour, and at 11 o'clock (10 on Sundays) the colourful ceremony of Changing the Guard takes place. Through the archway is Horse Guard's Parade, scene of the Trooping the Colour ceremony, which takes place annually on the Queen's official birthday, the second Saturday in June.

Almost opposite is the **Banqueting House**, the main surviving part of Whitehall Palace. It was built by Inigo Jones in 1619-22 in Palladian style. Charles I passed through a window of the hall to his execution in 1649. A staircase leads to the spacious Banqueting Hall, whose

The Life Guards

impressive ceiling was designed by Rubens. It was commissioned by Charles I and shows allegorical scenes glorifying the monarchy.

Further down on the right is **Downing Street**, closed off by a new gateway. The street is named after its builder, Sir George Downing, and contains the Prime Minister's residence at number 10 and that of the Chancellor of the Exchequer at number 11. The Cenotaph in the centre of Whitehall was designed by Lutyens and commemorates the dead of the two World Wars. A memorial ceremony is held here annually in the presence of the sovereign on Armistice Day in November, when wreaths are laid. Beyond the Cenotaph, Whitehall becomes Parliament Street and leads to Parliament Square.

At the end of King Charles Street on the right are the **Cabinet War Rooms**. These underground rooms, now open to the public, were used as emergency accommodation for Winston Churchill, the War Cabinet and the Chiefs of Staff during the Second World War. You can

see the Cabinet Room, the Transatlantic Telephone Room, which Churchill used to speak to President Roosevelt, the Map Room where information was collected, and the Prime Minister's Room, used by Churchill to make a number of his wartime speeches.

Trafalgar Square. Nelson's Column

Trooping the Colour. H.M. the Queen and Prince Philip and Prince of Wales.

Whitehall. The Horse Guards.

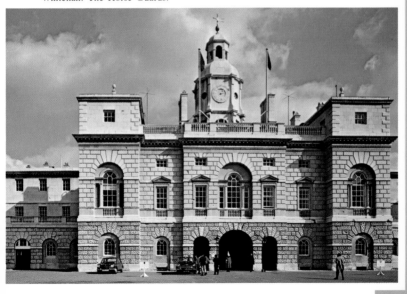

THIRD ITINERARY

WESTMINSTER CATHEDRAL - ROYAL MEWS - BUCKINGHAM PALACE - ST. JAMES'S PARK - LANCASTER HOUSE - ST. JAMES'S PALACE - MARLBOROUGH HOUSE - ST JAMES'S

Just outside busy Victoria Station, on a traffic island, stands "Little Ben", a clock modelled on the Clock Tower of the Houses of Parliament. It stood here from 1892 to 1964 and was re-erected in 1981. A short distance along Victoria Street, on the right, is a large piazza leading to **Westminster Cathedral**, the most important Roman Catholic church in Britain. It was designed in

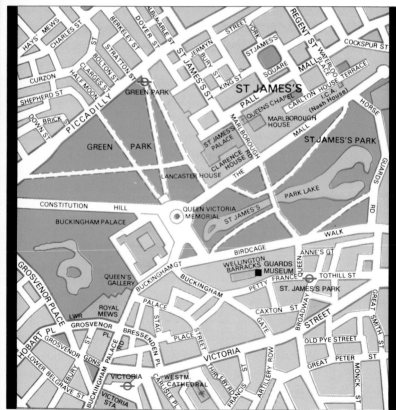

Neo-Byzantine style by J.F. Bentley and consecrated in 1910. The striking exterior has alternate bands of red brick and Portland stone and the bell-tower (St. Edward's Tower) is 284ft. high. The tympanum over the main door contains a mosaic by R. Anning Bell representing Christ, St. Peter, Edward the Confessor and the Virgin with St. Joseph. The interior is based on a basilica plan and boasts the widest nave in England. It is richly decorated with marble and mosaics, but the decoration is still incomplete. The two large columns of red Norwegian granite at the west end symbolize the Precious Blood of Christ.

Almost opposite the cathedral, Bressenden Place leads to Buckingham Gate and the **Royal Mews**, built by John

Westminster Cathedral.

BUCKINGHAM PALACE

Nash in 1826. Here you can see the Queen's coaches and horses when not in use for state occasions. The State Carriage (used for coronations) was designed for George III by Sir William Chambers and painted by Cipriani. Also on view are the Irish State Coach used for the State Opening of Parliament, the Glass State Coach used for royal weddings and the Australian State Coach, presented in 1988.

A short walk along Buckingham Gate is the **Queen's Gallery**, which holds changing exhibitions of works from the extensive royal collections.

Buckingham Palace and the Queen Victoria Memorial.

Buckingham Palace: Changing the Guard.

Buckingham Palace: the Royal Family

Continuing along Buckingham Gate you come to **Buckingham Palace**, with the Mall and St. James's Park stretching before it. Built in 1702-5 for the Duke of Buckingham, it was sold to George III in 1761, and George IV commissioned John Nash to remodel it. With the accession of Queen Victoria it became the sovereign's permanent London residence. The east front was remodelled in 1913 by Sir Aston Webb. Garden parties (by invitation only) are held every July in the extensive grounds of the palace, and when the sovereign is in residence the Royal Standard is flown from the masthead.

The colourful spectacle of **Changing the Guard** takes place in the forecourt at 11.30 (daily from April to August, on alternate days from mid-August to March. Check with the London Tourist Board for details). The Queen's Guard troop the Queen's colour from St. James's Palace, while the new guard, led by a military band, arrives from Wellington Barracks for the ceremony, which lasts for about 30 minutes, to the accompaniment of the band.

In front of the palace is the impressive Queen Victoria Memorial, designed by Sir Aston Webb and sculpted by Sir Thomas Brock in 1911. It shows the seated figure of the queen with groups portraying Truth, Justice and Motherhood, and it is crowned by the winged figure of Victory supported by Courage and Constancy.

St. James's Park, one of the most beautiful in London, was enclosed as a deer park by Henry VIII, laid out by Le Nôtre for Charles II and later redesigned by Nash for George IV. A lake extends for almost the whole length of the park, and there are fine views towards Westminster from its bridge. The park is renowned for the variety of its birds, in particular the pelicans. Bordering the park to the south is Birdcage Walk, where Charles II had his aviaries, with Wellington Barracks, the Guards' Chapel and the Guards' Museum, which illustrates the life and campaigns of the Foot Guards.

Along the north side of St. James's Park runs the Mall, which takes its name from the game of "paille-maille"

The Queen Victoria Memorial.

which was played here in Charles II's time. Overlooking the Mall are a number of impressive mansions. Starting from the western end, we first see **Lancaster House**. Originally called York House, the building was begun in 1825 by Benjamin Wyatt for the Duke of York, and completed in 1840 by Smirke and Barry for the Marquess of Stafford. It has magnificent state apartments with ceiling paintings by Guercino and Veronese, and an impressive double staircase by Barry. In 1912 it was sold to Sir William Lever (later first Viscount Leverhulme) who renamed it Lancaster House after his native county.

Lancaster House

He later gave the house to the nation and it housed the London Museum until 1946. The Coronation Banquet of Queen Elizabeth II was held here in 1953 and it now serves as a Government hospitality centre.

Just across Stable Yard is **Clarence House**, built in 1825 by Nash for William IV, then Duke of Clarence. It is now the home of the Queen Mother, and a piper plays at 9 every morning when she is in residence. Behind Clarence House is **St. James's Palace**, built on the site of a

St. James's Palace: the Tudor Gatehouse

THE QUEEN'S CHAPEL

former leper hospital dedicated to St. James the Less. The picturesque brick palace was built for Henry VIII and became the main royal residence after fire destroyed Whitehall Palace in 1698. Since 1837 Buckingham Palace has been the sovereign's London residence, but ambassadors are still accredited to the "Court of St. James's". Although the palace is not open to the public, visitors may attend services between October and Palm Sunday in the Chapel Royal, which boasts a superb ceiling attributed to Holbein.

Opposite the palace, in Marlborough Road, is the Queen's Chapel, designed in 1623 by Inigo Jones, originally for the Infanta Maria of Spain, Charles I's prospective bride, but completed for Henrietta Maria, whom he married in 1625. It is notable for its Carolean pews and panelling, as well as a fine coffered ceiling. Behind the chapel and set in spacious grounds, is **Marlborough House**. It was built in 1709-11 by Wren for the Duke of Marlborough, but the third storey was added later. The future George V was born here in 1865 and Queen Mary died here in 1953. In 1962 it became a Commonwealth conference and research centre.

Carlton House Terrace

◆ The Queen's Chapel

Marlborough House.

MARLBOROUGH HOUSE

Return to the Mall and continue left. Further along on this side is Carlton House Terrace, built by Nash in 1827-32 as mansions for the aristocracy, but now mostly used as offices. Located here are the Mall Galleries, which hold regular exhibitions, and the Institute of Contemporary Arts, which houses an art gallery, cinema and theatre. At the top of Duke of York Steps is the Duke of York's Column, designed by Wyatt and with a statue by Westmacott. It commemorates the second son of George III and Commander-in-Chief of the British army, better known as the "Grand Old Duke of York" who "had ten thousand men".

Beyond the monument is Waterloo Place, which contains a number of statues, including the Guards' Monument, with a statue of Florence Nightingale, the "lady with the lamp". The Athenaeum Club, with a copy of the Parthenon frieze running round it, stands on the corner of Pall Mall, a street famous for its clubs, among them

Buckingham Palace

the Travellers' Club, the Reform Club and the Royal Automobile Club. Just off Pall Mall, to the north, is St. James's Square, laid out in the 18th century by the first Earl of St. Albans. In the garden is an equestrian statue of William III, and Norfolk House (No. 31) was General Eisenhower's headquarters during the Second World War.

Pall Mall joins up with St. James's Street and there is a good view of the Tudor gateway of St. James's Palace. It was because of the royal residence that **St. James's** became fashionable and many smart shops and clubs opened here in the 18th century. Two of the most interesting of the old shops are the wine merchants Berry Bros. and Rudd at No. 3 and the hatters Lock & Co. at No. 6, who produced the first "bowler" hat. In King Street, on the right, is the famous auction house, Christie's. Further up St James's Street are three more famous clubs, Brook's (No. 60), Boodle's (No. 28) and White's (No. 37). White's is the oldest club in London, and started as a chocolate house in 1693. Continuing up St. James's Street you come to Piccadilly, which is covered in the next itinerary.

St. James's Park

FOURTH ITINERARY

PICCADILLY CIRCUS - PICCADILLY - ROYAL ACADEMY - MAYFAIR - APSLEY HOUSE - MARBLE ARCH - OXFORD STREET

Piccadilly Circus is one of London's busiest road junctions, always crowded with vehicles and people, popular because of the many theatres, shops and restaurants in the vicinity. It is most spectacular at night when all the brightly-coloured signs are lit up. It was laid out in the 19th century at the meeting point of several important streets, Piccadilly to the west, Regent Street sweeping north to Regent's Park, Shaftesbury Avenue leading to Soho and theatreland, and Coventry Street taking you eastwards to Leicester Square. In the centre, but now more accessible on a pedestrianised island, is the

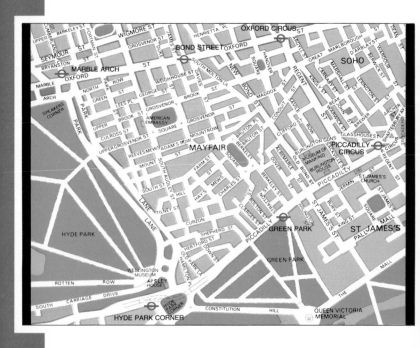

Shaftesbury Memorial, with the famous statue of Eros, more correctly the Angel of Christian Charity. The south side of the circus is currently being redeveloped, but the underground Criterion Theatre will be retained. On the north-east side is the London Pavilion built in 1885 as a theatre and later a cinema. It now houses a shopping complex and **Rock Circus**, an award-winning exhibition of the story of rock and pop music, using amazing new animatronic techniques. A short distance along Coventry Street is the Trocadero, which, as well as a variety of shops and eating places, houses the **Guinness World Of Records**, an exhibition based on the Guinness Book of Records. A wide variety of record-breakers are illustrated from the tallest man to space exploration.

Return to Piccadilly Circus and cross over to **Piccadilly**. The name comes from Piccadilly Hall, the name given to

The Shaftesbury Memorial.

the house of Robert Baker, a tailor who made his money from making "picadils", a kind of ruff or collar popular at the time. Piccadilly was once the main route to the west of England, and is now a busy road leading to the even busier Hyde Park Corner. (When crossing the road, watch out for the buses which travel against the traffic in their own lane).

A short way along on the left is the Church of St. James, built by Wren in 1676-84. It was badly damaged in the Second World War, but was well restored in 1954. It contains a fine barrel-vaulted ceiling and the font, altar-piece and organ case are all by the master-carver, Grinling Gibbons. Also on the left are Hatchards, the famous bookshop, and Fortnum and Mason, the well-known store, founded in 1770. A delightful mechanical clock over the entrance has figures of Mr Fortnum and Mr Mason who bow to each other on the hour.

On the other side of the street stands Burlington House, originally built as a mansion in 1665, but enlarged and rebuilt in the 18th century. It now houses the **Royal Academy of Arts** and a number of learned societies. The Royal Academy of Arts was founded in 1768, with Sir Joshua Reynolds as its first president, and was based at Somerset House and the National Gallery before moving here in 1869. Regular loan exhibitions are held here as well as the annual Summer Exhibition of new works by contemporary artists. The Academy's own collection includes works by Reynolds, Gainsborough and Constable as well as the Michelangelo tondo, an exquisite relief of the Virgin and Child.

Alongside Burlington House is the **Burlington Arcade**, a covered row of exclusive shops. It was built in 1819 by Samuel Ware for Lord George Cavendish, apparently to stop passers-bys throwing rubbish into his garden. It is

Piccadilly Circus

Burlington Arcade

still watched over by Beadles, who enforce rules against
running and singing. At the north end of the arcade, in
Burlington Gardens, is the **Museum of Mankind**, which
is the Ethnographical Department of the British
Museum. Its varied collection illustrates many cultures
from around the world. At the eastern end of Burlington

Gardens is Savile Row, famous for its bespoke tailors. To the west is Bond Street, with many exclusive shops and galleries. At No. 35 is Sotheby's, the famous auction house founded in 1744.

Riding in Hyde Park

You are now in **Mayfair**, which stretches west to Park Lane. The name comes from the fair held here annually in May until its suppression in the mid-18th century. Many impressive houses were built here in the 17th and

18th centuries, though many have now been turned into offices or clubs. There are a number of elegant squares, including Berkeley Square with its ample garden, and Grosvenor Square, dominated by the American Embassy.

Back on Piccadilly, the Ritz Hotel overlooks Green Park, where Handel's "Music for the Royal Fireworks" was first performed in 1749. Piccadilly continues along the side of the park to Hyde Park Corner, another busy road junction. On the island in the centre are a number of statues and monuments and the Wellington Arch, designed by Decimus Burton in 1828, crowned by Adrian Jones' bronze quadriga, erected in 1912.

Park Lane

On the north side of the island an equestrian statue of the Duke of Wellington faces **Apsley House**, the Wellington Museum, also known as "No. 1, London". The house was originally built in 1771-8 by Robert Adam for Baron Apsley, but it was later sold, first to Lord Wellesley, then, in 1817, to his brother, the Duke of Wellington, the victor of the Battle of Waterloo. The Duke had a number of changes made to the house, including the addition of the impressive Waterloo Gallery, where he

Auction at Sotheby's

held annual Waterloo Banquets from 1830 until his death. As well as containing much Wellington memorabilia, including medals, portraits and personal belongings, the house has several fine rooms and an

Hyde Park Corner.

Apsley House with the Wellington Statue to the left.

Marble Arch

Equestrian Statue of Wellington, with the Wellington Arch, crowned by a Statue of Peace, in the background

excellent collection of paintings, some bought by the Duke, others captured from the French after the Battle of Victoria and presented to the Duke by Ferdinand VII. There are works by Correggio, Rubens, Murillo and Velazquez, and an equestrian portrait of the Duke by Goya. In the staircase vestibule is Canova's colossal nude statue of Napoleon. There is also a large collection of porcelain, including Sèvres and Meissen, as well as the impressive Portuguese Service of silver and silver-gilt, presented to the Duke in 1816. North of the house, on the edge of Hyde Park, is Westmacott's statue of Achilles, erected in honour of Wellington and paid for by the "women of England".

Park Lane was once full of great mansions, but is now better known for its luxury hotels. At the north end is **Speakers' Corner**, where, on Sundays, orators are free to pronounce their opinions on almost any subject, usually to the accompaniment of much good-natured heck-

Hyde Park. The Serpentine.

ling. On a traffic island is **Marble Arch**, originally designed by Nash for Buckingham Palace, but moved here in 1850. Close by is the site of Tyburn, the infamous

Oxford Street with Selfridge's Store.

gallows where public executions were carried out until 1783. Stretching eastwards from Marble Arch is Oxford Street, London's best known shopping street, with its many department stores and smaller shops.

5

FIFTH
ITINERARY

HYDE PARK - KENSINGTON GARDENS - KENSINGTON PALACE - LEIGHTON HOUSE - ALBERT MEMORIAL - ROYAL ALBERT HALL - SCIENCE MUSEUM - NATURAL HISTORY MUSEUM - VICTORIA & ALBERT MUSEUM - BROMPTON ORATORY - KNIGHTSBRIDGE - CHELSEA

Hyde Park once belonged to the manor of Hyde, the property of Westminster Abbey, but after the Dissolution of the Monasteries Henry VIII turned it into a deerpark. In 1635 it was opened to the public and it became a fashionable place to be seen in, though later it became the haunt of robbers and many duels were fought here. In 1851 the Great Exhibition was held on the south side of the park. The famous Crystal Palace, designed specially for the exhibition by Joseph Paxton, was later

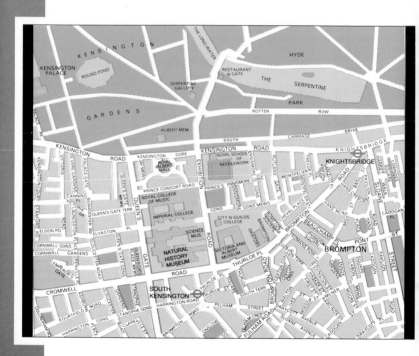

moved to Sydenham in south London, where it burnt
down in 1936. Running along the south of the park is a
mile-long horse-riding track called Rotten Row (a cor-
ruption of Route du Roi). It is possible to hire boats on
the Serpentine, an artificial lake created in the 18th
century by damming the Westbourne stream.

To the west the park becomes **Kensington Gardens**,
which were once the private park of Kensington Palace.
The gardens, with their avenues of trees, were originally
laid out by Charles Bridgeman in 1728-31 for Queen
Caroline, wife of George II. To the north of the park, by
the lake (here called the Long Water), is Frampton's

Kensington Gardens: Statue of Peter Pan

KENSINGTON PALACE

famous statue of Peter Pan, the hero of J.M. Barrie's well known play. In the centre is the Round Pond, now usually full of model boats.

Just west of the Round Pond is **Kensington Palace**. Originally built for the first Earl of Nottingham, it was bought

Kensington Palace

Kensington Palace: the Sunken Garden

in 1689 by William III, who needed to live away from Whitehall for his health. Sir Christopher Wren was employed to modify the house, and splendid gardens were laid out. Later alterations were carried out for George I by Colen Campbell and William Kent. Queen Victoria was born here and she lived here until her accession to the throne in 1837, when she moved to Buckingham Palace. Members of the Royal Family still live in the palace.

On the ground floor is the Court Dress Collection, which consists of dresses and uniforms worn at court from 1750 to the present day, and also includes the wedding dress of the Princess of Wales. The State Apartments on the first floor begin with Queen Mary's apartments, including the Bedchamber, which contains James II's State Bed, complete with its original hangings. There then follow a number of state rooms decorated by William Kent. The unusual ceiling in the Presence Chamber is in the Pompeian style, while the walls and ceiling of the Grand Staircase are painted with a trompe l'oeil scene of a crowded gallery. The King's Gallery is hung with a collection of 17th century paintings, including Rubens' Satyrs and Sleeping Nymphs. Above the fireplace is an unusual wind-dial made for William III, which still works. Queen Victoria's Bedroom is the room in which she awoke in 1837 to find she was Queen. The King's Council Chamber contains exhibits from the Great Exhibition in 1851, including an ivory throne presented to Queen Victoria by the Maharajah of Travancore. The Cupola Room, lavishly decorated by Kent, was the main state room of the palace, and is where Queen Victoria was baptised.

In the grounds of the palace are the delightful Sunken Garden, an impressive Orangery built for Queen Anne, and a statue of Queen Victoria sculpted by her daughter, Princess Louise.

Leaving the park in the south-west corner, turn right into Kensington High Street. In Stafford Terrace, off Argyll Street on the right, is **Linley Sambourne House**, a well-preserved upper-middle-class Victorian house maintained by the Victorian Society. Further along Kensington High Street is the Commonwealth Institute, an exhibition hall illustrating aspects of countries of the Commonwealth. At 12 Holland Park Road is **Leighton House**, built in 1866 by the artist, Lord Leighton. As well as a collection of paintings by the Pre-Raphaelites and Lord Leighton himself, the house contains the astonishing Arab Hall, with its fountain, and decorated with 14th-16th century Persian tiles. To the north is Holland Park with the remains of Holland House, a Jacobean mansion badly damaged in the last war.

Return to Kensington Road where, on the south side of Kensington Gardens, stands the **Albert Memorial**, currently shrouded in scaffolding while it undergoes extensive repairs. It was designed by George Gilbert Scott and unveiled by Queen Victoria in 1876 as a tribute to her beloved consort, Prince Albert. He is seen sitting under a "Gothic" canopy, holding a catalogue of the Great Exhibition of which he was the enthusiastic promoter, and around the sides of the monument are marble reliefs of notable men of the arts and sciences. At the corners are allegorical groups representing Agriculture, Commerce, Manufacturing and Engineering.

The Albert Memorial

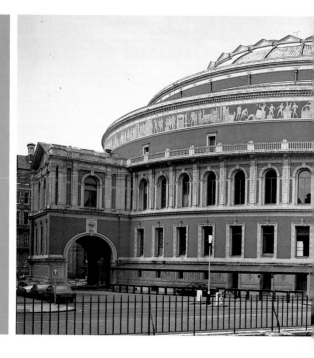

ALBERT MEMORIAL

The Great Exhibition was such a success that 88 acres of land south of Hyde Park were bought with the profits, and here were founded a number of institutions for the study of the arts and sciences. Among these were the museums we will shortly be visiting and, directly opposite the Albert Memorial, the **Royal Albert Hall**. Built in 1867-71 to the design of Captain Fowke, the hall is in the form of a huge amphitheatre and is covered with a glass and iron dome. The terracotta Minton frieze below the cornice illustrates the Triumph of the Arts & Sciences. The hall can seat up to 8000 people and is used for a variety of sporting events, banquets, balls and concerts, the best known of which are the Henry Wood Promenade Concerts which take place from July to September each year. The famous Willis organ, one of the biggest in Britain, was first played by Anton Bruckner at the inaugural concert. Tours of the hall are available in the summer months.

The Royal Albert Hall

SCIENCE MUSEUM

Walk down Exhibition Road and you will shortly come to the **Science Museum**, founded in 1856 to illustrate the history and application of scientific discovery and invention.

On the ground floor are impressive steam engines, the exploration of space and a display of road and rail vehicles. In the basement are domestic appliances and the popular Children's Gallery, with lots of buttons to push. Children will also enjoy Launch Pad on the first floor, where they are encouraged to play with the exhibits. Also on this floor are telecommunications, meteorology and a new exhibition about what we eat called Food for Thought. The second floor includes a fine collection of model ships and marine engines. On the third floor is the impressive Aeronautics collection, which includes the plane in which Alcock and Brown made the first non-stop transatlantic flight. Also on this floor are displays on photography and optics (including holography and lasers).

The fourth and fifth floors contain the splendid Wellcome Museum of the History of Medicine. On the lower floor are a number of tableaux and dioramas illustrating the history of medicine, nursing and dentistry. The upper floor is a display of the Science and Art of Medicine, which covers the subject from pre-Christian times and includes many cultures other than our own. Exhibits include Napoleon's toothbrush and Dr Livingstone's medicine chest.

A short walk down Exhibition Road brings you to the Earth Galleries of the **Natural History Museum** (until recently the Geological Museum). The main entrance is in Cromwell Road, and from here you can fully appreciate the magnificent building, which opened in 1881. It was designed by Alfred Waterhouse in Romanesque style, and the terracotta panels are decorated, both inside and out, with sculptures of plants and animals. The museum originated with the collection of Sir Hans Sloane, and later material came from the expeditions of Captain Cook and Charles Darwin. Although some of the older display cases still remain, most of the galleries now use films, working models and computers to bring their subjects to life.

NATURAL HISTORY MUSEUM

The spacious Central Hall houses a display on Dinosaurs and is dominated by the skeleton of Diplodocus. In the galleries to the left are displays of birds, insects and marine invertebrates. Look out for the dodo and the case of humming-birds, which is the oldest display in the museum. The Discovering Mammals display includes the famous life-size model of the Blue Whale. The Human Biology exhibition uses modern techniques to explain the workings of the human mind and body. On the first floor are exhibitions about man's place in evolution, the Origin of the Species and a fine collection of minerals, rocks and meteorites. The second floor is devoted to British natural history.

Return to the ground floor and make your way to the Earth Galleries. Here there is a display telling the Story of the Earth from its formation to the present day. It includes a piece of lunar rock and a simulation of an earthquake. Treasures of the Earth explains how minerals are extracted and illustrates their many uses. In the main hall is a splendid display of gemstones and on the mezzanine floor is an exhibition of British Fossils.

The Whale Room

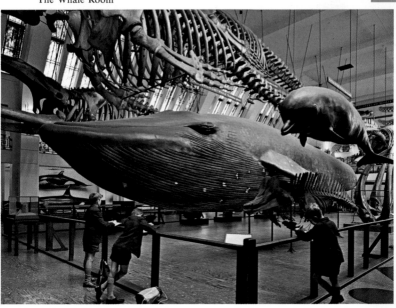

Natural History Museum

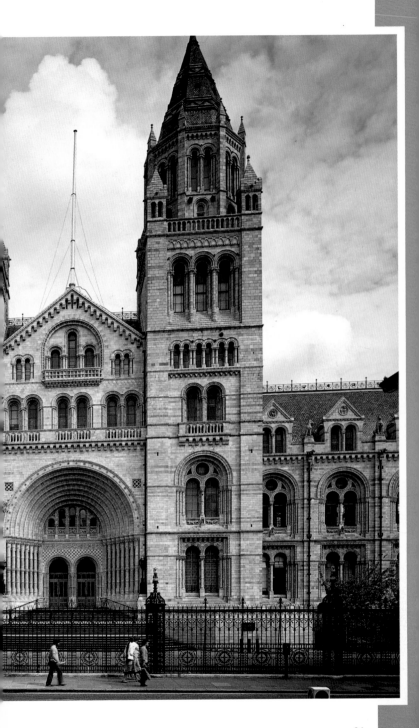

VICTORIA & ALBERT MUSEUM

Across Exhibition Road is the **Victoria & Albert Museum**, which houses one of the world's finest collections of the decorative arts. It began in 1852 as the Museum of Manufactures based at Marlborough House, and moved to its present site in 1857, when it was known as the South Kensington Museum. It soon outgrew the old building and in 1899 Queen Victoria laid the foundation stone of the present building, designed by Aston Webb. It was reopened in 1909 as the Victoria & Albert Museum, now more familiarly known as the "V & A".

The museum is vast and confusing, with 8 miles of galleries, so do not try to see too much at once. At the information desk just inside the entrance you can pick up a free plan, ask about any galleries that many be closed or arrange to go on a free introductory tour. The collections are divided into two main groups. The Art and Design galleries bring together different types of art by period or geographical area. The Materials and Techniques galleries specialise in particular types of object and are mainly on the upper floors.

A good place to start a visit is the Medieval Treasury in Room 43, just behind the main foyer. Here is displayed a magnificent collection of European art from 400 to 1400, including enamels, ivories, stained glass, illustrated manuscripts and textiles. Among the many beautiful objects are the ivory Symmachi Panel (Roman, c. 400), the Gloucester Candlestick (English, 12th century), the Eltenberg Reliquary in the shape of a church (Cologne, 12th century) and the Syon Cope (English, 14th century). Rooms 22-24 beyond cover Gothic Art from 1100-1450, with many wood and stone carvings including Pisano's bust of the prophet Haggai. Room 25 is dominated by the splendid 15th century St George altarpiece from Valencia in Spain. Rooms 26-29 are given over to the Renaissance in Northern Europe, with carvings, metalwork, textiles and a fine collection of Limoges enamel. Look out for the German Castle Cup and the silver Burghley Nef, a 16th century French salt-cellar in the form of a ship balanced on a mermaid.

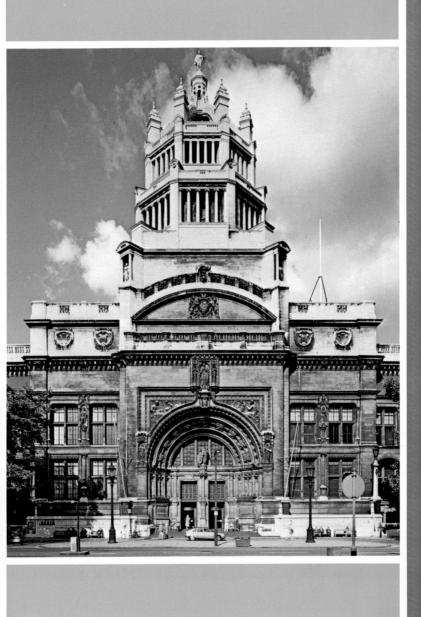

The Victoria and Albert Museum, Exterior

Victoria and Albert Museum: Devonshire Hunting Tapestry

Rooms 11-20 contain an exceptionally fine display of Italian Renaissance art, particularly strong in sculpture, metalwork, majolica and church furniture. The most important works in Room 16 are by the Florentine sculptor Donatello, including the low relief Ascension with Christ Giving the Keys to Peter and the Cellini Tondo or Virgin and Child with Angels. In Room 15 is Duccio's marble relief of the Virgin and Child with Angels, and Room 13 contains terracotta sculpture by the della Robbia family.

From Rooms 15 and 13 you can visit the impressive Morris, Gamble and Poynter Rooms, the original refreshment rooms of the museum. William Morris and Philip Webb designed the Morris Room and Burne-Jones designed the glass and painted panels. The Poynter Room is decorated with tiles painted by pupils of the Royal College of Art.

Victoria and Albert Museum: Indian Statue

Victoria and Albert Museum: Raphael Cartoon of the Miracle of the Fishes

Room 12 contains a number of bronzes, including the Shouting Horseman by Riccio. Turning left, Room 17 has an early 16th century ceiling from Cremona, and there are a number of Verrocchio sculptures in Room 18. Note also a fine 16th century pearwood altarpiece from Piedmont in Room 20. Rooms 21 and 21A contain European art of the 16th century. Note Giambologna's powerful marble statue of Samson Slaying a Philistine, and, in a display cabinet, a small wax model of a Slave by Michelangelo.

To continue the sequence of European art, take the stairs down to the left at the end of Room 21. In Room 1A is a beautifully decorated spinet by Annibale dei Rossi, and Room 1C contains busts by Algardi and Bernini as well as a cabinet belonging to Marie de Medici. Room 2 contains fine silverware, and Room 3B has a panelled room from the hunting-lodge of King Henry IV of France. Room 4 has a fine collection of Meissen porcelain, and Room 5 contains 17th century French furniture, porcelain and paintings. In Room 6 are some fine Limoges enamels and a jewel casket belonging to the Empress Maria Theresa. In Room 7 is the Cabinet (or Boudoir) of Madame de Sérilly and Sèvres porcelain. Cross the entrance hall to reach the last two rooms in this sequence. Room 8 covers European and American Art from 1800-1890 and includes furniture shown at the Great Exhibition in 1851. Room 9 contains Art Nouveau furniture, glassware and posters. In Room 50, to the right of the foyer, is a display of British and European sculpture. Rooms 46A and 46B beyond hold an extraordinary collection of Victorian plaster casts, among them full-size copies of Trajan's Column and Michelangelo's David. The new Toshiba Gallery of Japanese Art includes fine collections of lacquer and netsuke. Room 42 contains an impressive display of the Art of Islam, and next door, in Room 41, is the Nehru Gallery of Indian Art. Room 40 houses the Dress Collection, illustrating fashionable clothes from 1600 to the present day. Above, in Room 40A, is a superb collection of musical instruments, most of them highly decorated.

Room 48 contains the magnificent Raphael Cartoons. They are full-scale designs for tapestries on the lives of Saints Peter and Paul, commissioned from Raphael by Pope Leo X in 1515. These seven cartoons were bought in 1623 by Prince Charles, later Charles I, and were loaned to the V & A by Queen Victoria. The original tapestries hang in the Vatican Museum.

A fascinating sequence of galleries illustrating British Art and Design begins in Room 52, which houses Queen Elizabeth's virginals and the Oxburgh Hangings, embroidered by Mary, Queen of Scots. Room 54 contains the famous Great Bed of Ware, a vast carved oak bed mentioned by Shakespeare in Twelfth Night. Room 55 displays an exquisite cravat carved in limewood by Grinling Gibbons, and Room 58 contains the beautiful 18th century music room from Norfolk House.
On the stairs up to the next floor hang a number of paintings from Vauxhall Gardens. Room 125 contains bookcases from Croome Court by Robert Adam and part of the Glass Drawing Room from Northumberland House (also by Adam). Room 123 houses the Lee Priory Room in Strawberry Hill Gothic by James Wyatt, while Room 122 contains furniture by Chippendale and the Adam ceiling from David Garrick's room in Adelphi

5

Terrace. Rooms 120-118 cover the Victorian Age, with
an extensive display of furniture, paintings and sculpture. Take the stairs down to Room 74, which houses a
display of the 20th century up to 1960, including work by
Mackintosh, Lutyens, Vanessa Bell, Duncan Grant and
Eric Gill.

Return to the ground floor and make your way to the
Henry Cole Wing. On this level is an excellent restaurant. On level 4 is a superb collection of English portrait
miniatures, with particularly fine examples by Holbein,
Hilliard and Oliver. On the same level is a gallery of 19th
century paintings, including a fine view of Venice by
Turner and works by Fuseli, Landseer and Millet. On
level 6 is a large and splendid collection of paintings and
sketches by Constable, including Salisbury Cathedral
and full-scale sketches for the Haywain and the Leaping
Horse. As you leave the museum by the Exhibition
Road exit you will see a number of Rodin bronzes presented by the sculptor in 1914.

Next to the museum in Brompton Road stands the
Brompton Oratory, or the Oratory of St Philip Neri. This
Roman Catholic church was designed in ornate Italian
baroque style by Herbert Gribble and completed in
1884, though the dome was not added until 1896.

Brompton Oratory

Brompton Road leads north-east to meet the elegant shopping area of Knightsbridge, where the stylish boutiques and stores are dominated by Harrods department store. Founded in 1849 as a small grocery shop by Henry Harrod, the store has become synonymous with luxury and is famous for its range of goods and services, including a pet shop, restaurants, the famous Food Halls and a Tourist Information Centre.

From the corner of Knightsbridge, Sloane Street stretches southwards to Sloane Square. Here is the Royal Court Theatre, where many of Shaw's plays and John Osborne's Look Back in Anger were first performed. West of Sloane Square, Chelsea has been a fashionable area since Tudor times, when Henry VIII used to visit Sir Thomas More at his home here. In the 19th century it was popular with the Pre-Raphaelite Brotherhood. It was particularly fashionable during the "Swinging Sixties" and is still a centre for fashionable shops. In Royal Hospital Road is the **Royal Hospital, Chelsea**, where the Chelsea Flower Show is held each May. The hospital, which serves as a hospice for old and disabled soldiers, was the brainchild of Charles II, who was inspired by the Hôtel des Invalides in Paris, a similar project conceived by Louis XIV in 1670. Between 400-500 old soldiers, known as the Chelsea Pensioners, now live here and are easily recognisable by their traditional long coats, scarlet in summer and blue in winter. The building was designed by Sir Christopher Wren, though some later alterations were carried out by Robert Adam and Sir John Soane.

Further down Royal Hospital Road is the **National Army Museum**, which records the history of the British Army from 1485 to 1982, by means of uniforms, weapons, medals and personal relics. There are also a number of portraits by Reynolds, Romney and Lawrence. Continuing down Royal Hospital Road you pass Tite Street, once home to the artists Augustus John and Whistler and the writer, Oscar Wilde. At the junction with the Chelsea Embankment is the **Chelsea Physic Garden**, established in the 17th century. In 1723 it was presented to the Society of Apothecaries by Sir Hans Sloane, whose statue, by Rysbrack, stands in the centre of the garden.

Harrod's Store

CHELSEA

Chelsea Embankment offers views of Albert and Chelsea Bridges, and, across the Thames, of Battersea Park with the Peace Pagoda, and further downstream, of the former Battersea Power Station, whose future is still uncertain. Further west is Cheyne Walk with a number of delightful Georgian houses – the writer George Eliot

Monument to Thomas More

died at No. 4 in 1880, and Dante Gabriel Rossetti, along with an infamous menagerie, lived at No. 16. In Cheyne Row is **Carlyle's House**, where the writer Thomas Carlyle and his wife lived from 1834. It is now looked after by the National Trust and remains very much as it was in Carlyle's time, to the extent that there is no electricity. At the end of Cheyne Walk is **Chelsea Old Church**, which was founded in the 12th century. It was extensively damaged in the last war and was rebuilt in 1958. Fortunately, the 14th century More Chapel, which was rebuilt in 1528 by Sir Thomas More, survived the bombing. More lived in Chelsea from 1524 until his dispute with Henry VIII over the break with Rome led to his imprisonment and execution in 1535. Henry VIII is reputed to have secretly married Jane Seymour in the Lawrence Chapel several days before the official ceremony.

Royal Hospital, Chelsea

The Thames at Chelsea

Further west is **Crosby Hall**, now occupied by the British Federation of University Women. Originally it was the great hall of Crosby Place, a mansion erected in the 15th century in Bishopsgate in the City of London. The house was lived in by the Duke of Gloucester, later Richard III, and was bought in 1523 by Sir Thomas More for his son-in-law. The hall was moved here in 1910 and retains a fine oak roof and its original oriel window. It also contains a copy of Holbein's painting of Sir Thomas More and his family.

SIXTH ITINERARY

REGENT STREET - WALLACE COLLECTION - MADAME TUSSAUD'S - LONDON PLANETARIUM - REGENT'S PARK - LONDON ZOO

Regent Street was laid out by John Nash between 1813 and 1825 as part of his grand design connecting the Prince Regent's residence, Carlton House, with Regent's Park. All the buildings have since been rebuilt and the street now houses many shops, including the

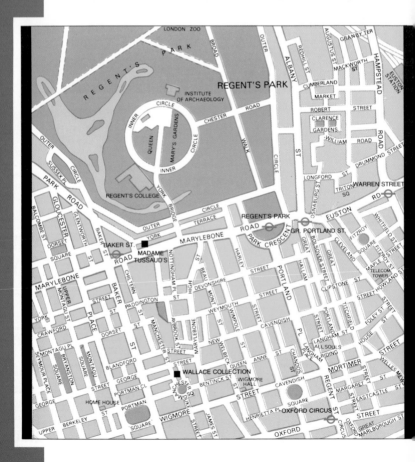

Liberty's Store

famous toy shop, Hamley's, and the unusual mock-Tudor building of Liberty's. Regent Street crosses Oxford Street at Oxford Circus and continues north to Langham Place, where the nerve centre of BBC Radio, Broadcasting House, stands opposite Nash's All Souls' Church. In Scala Street, a short walk to the east, Pollock's Toy Museum has an interesting collection of toys and toy theatres. In nearby Howland Street rises the 620ft. London Telecom Tower which opened in 1964. For security reasons the viewing platform is closed to the public.

Just south of Langham Place, Wigmore Street leads west from Cavendish Square, passing, on the right, the Wigmore Hall, used for concerts and recitals, and, on the left, the attractive shopping street, St. Christopher's Place. Further west, Duke Street leads north to Manchester Square and Hertford House, home of the magnificent **Wallace Collection**. The collection is particularly strong in 18th century French paintings, furniture and porcelain, but also includes fine Dutch paintings and an excellent display of arms and armour. It was formed by the Marquesses of Hertford in the 18th and 19th centuries, and was added to by Sir Richard Wallace, son of the 4th Marquess. On his death in 1897 Lady Wallace bequeathed the collection to the nation.

Room 1 contains 18th and 19th century English pictures and Louis XVI furniture, while Room 2 has displays of Sèvres porcelain and boulle furniture. Room 3 contains a varied display of objets d'art, including fine collections of Limoges enamel, illustrated manuscripts and wax portraits. Note also, above the fireplace, Torrigiani's Head of Christ, and, in a case on the east wall, the tiny French enamelled gold triptych from about 1500. In Room 4 are good displays of earthenware, coins, ivories and jewellery. Rooms 5-7 house a superb collection of European arms and armour, while Room 8 contains a fine display of Oriental arms and armour along with a number of 19th century French paintings of oriental scenes. Room 10 has a display of paintings by Bonington, and in the following corridor are watercolours by Bonington and Turner. Rooms 11 and 12 contain French furniture, paintings and sculpture of the 17th and 18th centuries.

Returning to the entrance hall, the staircase boasts a fine iron and bronze balustrade made for the Palais Mazarin in Paris. On the staircase walls and the top landing are impressive displays of paintings by Boucher. In Rooms 13 and 14 are several superb paintings of Venetian scenes by Canaletto and Guardi. Rooms 15-18 offer a fine collection of Flemish and Dutch paintings of the 17th century. It includes several Rubens sketches, and paintings by Hobbema, Ruisdael, Cuyp, Steen and van de Velde. Room 19, the Picture Gallery, is the magnificent setting for the finest paintings in the collection. Among them are Perseus and Andromeda by Titian, Dance to the Music of Time by Poussin, the Rainbow Landscape by Rubens, Nellie O'Brien by Reynolds, Rembrandt's portrait of his son, Titus, and Frans Hals' Laughing Cavalier. Room 20 contains a display of French 19th century painting, including Delacroix' Execution of the Doge. In Room 21 is a fine display of French 18th century painting and furniture. There are several works by Watteau including The Music Party and

Hertford House

Gilles and his Family, and Fragonard is also well represented, with the delightful Gardens of the Villa d'Este at Tivoli and his famous The Swing. The furniture includes several pieces made for Marie-Antoinette. In Room 22 are paintings by Boucher, including a portrait of Mme de Pompadour. Room 23 contains several sentimental 18th century paintings, including Reynolds' Miss Bowles. There is a fine display of snuffboxes in the corridor leading to Rooms 24 and 25, which contain several pieces of sculpture, including a bust by Houdon of Mme de Sérilly, whose boudoir can now be seen in the Victoria & Albert Museum.

Fitzhardinge Street leads from Manchester Square to Portman Square where, at No. 20, is Home House, one of Robert Adam's finest town houses. Next door is the

Wallace Collection, Fragonard: The Swing

Home House

6

MADAME TUSSAUD'S

Heinz Gallery of the Royal Institute of British Architects, which houses special exhibitions.

Baker Street, home of Conan Doyle's fictional detective, Sherlock Holmes, leads north from Portman Square to Marylebone Road and the wax museum, **Madame Tussaud's**. A self-portrait of Madame Tussaud can be seen in the entrance hall. She began her career making wax figures at the court of Louis XVI in France and after the outbreak of the French Revolution made death masks of victims of the guillotine, some of which are still on display. In 1802 she came to England where she took her exhibition all round the country before settling in London. The present building opened in 1884. As well as historical figures, the collection is constantly being updated to include new celebrities and political figures. Particularly popular is the Chamber of Horrors. Next door is the **London Planetarium** which offers

Madame Tussaud's Waxworks: Henry VIII and Anne Boleyn

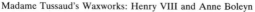

astronomical shows by day and laser light shows in the evening.

St. Marylebone Church, built by Thomas Hardwick in 1813-17 stands opposite York Gate which leads into **Regent's Park**. The park, which covers 472 acres, was laid out by Nash as part of his grand plan for the Prince Regent, and is surrounded by fine Regency terraces. Within the Inner Circle is the Open Air Theatre and the beautiful Queen Mary's Gardens. To the north the **London Zoo** occupies about 36 acres of the park. The Zoological Society was founded in 1826 and Decimus Burton designed the original enclosures. Some of these remain, but a programme of improvements is now being carried out. The Regent's Canal passes through the northern part of the Zoo and it is a pleasant place to walk. It is also possibile to take a boat trip to Little Venice or Camden Lock.

Planetarium and Mme Tussaud's

Regent's Park
London Zoo.

Regent's Canal

6

British Museum

BRITISH MUSEUM - BLOOMSBURY - PERCIVAL DAVID FOUNDATION - THOMAS CORAM FOUNDATION - DICKENS HOUSE - GRAY'S INN

The **British Museum** was founded in 1753, when it consisted of the newly acquired collection of Sir Hans Sloane together with manuscripts from the Cottonian Library and the manuscript collection of the Earl of Oxford. In 1755 Montague House in Bloomsbury was bought to house the museum and it opened to the public in 1759. The collections grew quickly, and with acquisitions such as the Elgin Marbles and George III's library, more space was soon needed.

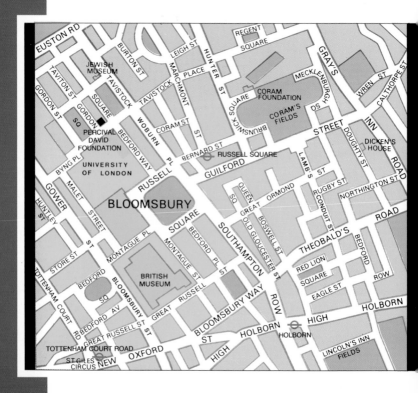

The present building was designed in imposing Classical style by Robert Smirke and was built between 1823-50, the famous domed Reading Room being added in 1857. Further extensions have been added over the years, and the Natural History and Ethnographical collections have been moved to separate sites. The British Library, now run separately from the Museum, is due to move in 1993 to more spacious premises in St. Pancras.

There is far too much to take in in one visit to the British Museum, so do not try to see too much at once. Pick up a free map of the galleries at the information desk just inside the main entrance, or perhaps you could take one of the tours.

British Museum: the Elgin Marbles in the Duveen Galiery: Fragments of the Frieze and East Pediment Group from the Parthenon

Rooms 1-15, starting to the left of the main entrance, house an extensive collection of Greek and Roman antiquities. Rooms 1 & 2 represent the early Cycladic, Minoan and Mycenaean periods, while Room 3 covers the Archaic period, with some splendid Athenian black-figured vases. In Room 5 are a number of lively red-figured vases from the 5th century BC and a lovely drinking cup showing Aphrodite riding a goose. Also

British Museum: Battle of the Lapiths and Centaurs from the Parthenon

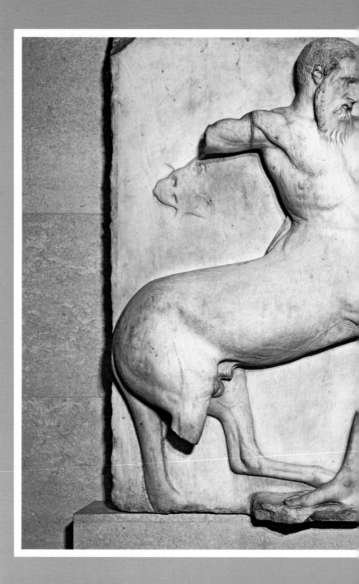

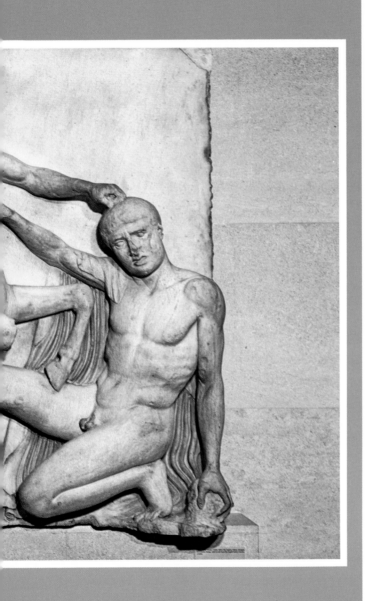

DUVEEN GALLERY

here are some fine reliefs from the Harpy Tomb at Xanthos. Up the stairs to the right in Room 6 is the splendid frieze from the Temple of Apollo at Bassae. Room 7 contains sculptures from the Nereid Monument, whose facade has been rebuilt at the far end of the gallery.

Room 8, to the left, is the Duveen Gallery, built specially to house the Elgin Marbles, sculptures from the Parthenon in Athens brought back by Lord Elgin between 1801-6. They consist of a long frieze portraying the Panathenaic procession, 15 of the original 92 metopes carved with battle scenes, and the East & West Pediment sculptures showing scenes from the life of Athena.

Detail of the East Pediment Group from the Elgin Marbles.

Room 9 contains a caryatid from the Erechtheion, and in Room 10 is the Tomb of Payava from Xanthos. Room 12 boasts sculptures from two of the Seven Wonders of the Ancient World, the Mausoleum at Halicarnassus and the Temple of Artemis at Ephesus. Room 13 moves into the Hellenistic period, with the famous Demeter of Cnidos and a bronze head of Sophocles. Also note some delightful small sculptures, including one of Eros riding a duck. Rooms 14 & 15 contain Roman art, with statues, silverwork and the outstanding Portland Vase of blue and white glass cut like a cameo.

In the basement the Wolfson Galleries house an extensive collection of Greek and Roman sculpture. Rooms 83-85 contain some particularly fine Roman sculpture, including the remarkable collection of Charles Townley in Room 84 and a superb display of portrait busts in Room 85. Rooms 68-73 on the first floor complete the Greek and Roman collection. In Room 68 is a display of bronzes and terracottas, while Room 69 illustrates aspects of daily life in Greece and Rome. Room 71 is devoted to Italy before the Roman Empire, with particular emphasis on the Etruscans, including a fine selection of engraved bronze mirrors. In Room 72 is a display on Cyprus, and Room 73, covering the Greeks in Southern Italy, includes a fine collection of pottery.

Several galleries on the ground floor are devoted to Assyrian antiquities. In Room 21 are reliefs from the palaces of Ashurbanipal and Sennacherib at Ninevah, and Room 19 contains reliefs from the palace of Ashurnasirpal II at Nimrud. Room 16 is dominated by two huge winged, human-headed bulls from Khorsabad. On no account miss Room 17, which contains the superb lion hunt reliefs from the palace of Ashurbanipal at Ninevah. There are further Assyrian reliefs in Rooms 88a and 89 in the basement. There are a number of rooms on the first floor which also contain antiquities from Western Asia. Rooms 51 & 52 contain displays on Iran and Anatolia. In the Iranian room is the Oxus Treasure with fine gold and silver objects, including two bracelets decorated with griffins. Also of note is a display of very sophisticated Sassanian silverware.

ANCIENT EGYPTIAN ART

British Museum: the Rosetta Stone

The Ancient Egyptian displays start in Room 25 on the ground floor. Just inside on the left is the Rosetta Stone whose text, in hieroglyphs, demotic Egyptian and Greek, proved to be the key to understanding hieroglyphic writing. In the first side gallery is a charming tomb painting from Thebes of Nebamun hunting wildfowl. Back in the main gallery note the huge granite head of Amenophis III and the delightful statue of a seated couple. In the central section of the gallery are displays of smaller objects, including a superb bronze cat with gold nose-ring and earrings. Beyond this is the colossal head of Rameses II in two-coloured granite. In another side room you will find the stunning gilded inner coffin of Henutmehit and the large sarcophagus of a priest, carved with a religious procession around the side. A walk up the stairs at the end of the gallery brings you to Rooms 60-64 where the Egyptian story continues. Rooms 60-61 house an amazing collection of coffins,

British Museum: Painting from the Tomb of Nebamun

EUROPEAN PREHISTORY

mummies and mummy cases, many of them colourfully decorated. Amongst them are several animal mummies, including cats and birds. In Room 62 are papyri, wall-paintings and amazingly life-like mummy paintings. Room 63 covers aspects of daily life and in Room 64 are displays of small bronzes and ivories.

Rooms 37-39 on the first floor are devoted to European Prehistory. In Room 37 is Bronze Age gold and pottery as well as the remains of Lindow Man, who apparently died the victim of a ritual killing. In Room 38 note two bronze wine flagons, superb examples of early Celtic craftsmanship. Room 39 has a fine collection of Celtic art, including weapons, pottery and jewellery. In particular note the Battersea Shield, a beautifully decorated bronze mirror and a display of gold torcs, or neck-rings.

The floor of Room 35 is covered by a large Roman mosaic from Hinton St. Mary, with the earliest known mosaic representation of Christ. Room 40 beyond has a remarkable collection of objects from Roman Britain, including jewellery, pottery, glassware and wall paintings. The finest display is of the 28 pieces of silver tableware known as the Mildenhall Treasure.

The Medieval Galleries begin in Room 41, which contains works of art from the 4th to the 11th centuries. The most famous objects are the Sutton Hoo ship burial display, especially the silver bowls and gold jewellery, but do stop to look at the whalebone Franks Casket and the amazing glass Lycurgus Cup. Room 42 covers the period from the 9th to the 15th centuries, with fine examples of Byzantine, Carolingian, Romanesque and Gothic art. Here are the famous ivory Lewis Chessmen, the beatiful gold and enamel Dunstable Swan Jewel and a gittern exquisitely carved in boxwood. The highlight of the room, however, is the dazzling gold and enamel Royal Gold Cup. Room 43 has a display of medieval tiles and pottery, while Room 44 is devoted to clocks and watches, including the extraordinary nef, or ship-clock made in 1580 for the Emperor Rudolf II. Room 45 houses the Waddesdon Bequest, which contains superb Medieval silver plate, maiolica, jewellery and enamels.

One of the finest pieces is the miniature Flemish altar-piece intricately carved from boxwood.
The Oriental collections are mostly housed in the northern part of the museum, though some of the galleries are being refurbished. The John Addis Islamic Gallery in Room 34 has fine collections of pottery, coins, tiles, glassware and brass. The Japanese Galleries (Rooms 92-94) are used for mounting changing exhibitions. Also in this building are the Prints and Drawings rooms, used for special exhibitions, but containing on permanent display Michelangelo's cartoon for Epifania.

The **British Library** Reading Room is beyond the main entrance to the museum. Under its vast dome are rows and rows of books which have attracted readers as diverse as Dickens, Shaw and Marx. A reader's pass is needed to study here, but visitors are briefly allowed in at set times. To the right of the main entrance are more rooms with displays from the British Library collections. There are many manuscripts of historical, literary and artistic importance, including Beowulf, the Gutenberg Bible, the Lindisfarne Gospels and two copies of the Magna Carta. In the King's Library, a splendid room specially built to house the library of George II, are a number of Shakespearean documents, including a First Folio.

Behind the British Museum is the area of **Bloomsbury**, which lent its name to the "Bloomsbury Group" of writers, intellectuals and artists, including Virginia Woolf and Lytton Strachey, who gathered here at the beginning of this century. Bloomsbury is also the site of many departments of the University of London, including the imposing Senate House in Malet Street. In Gordon Square to the north the **Percival David Foundation of Chinese Art** houses a fine collection of Chinese ceramics donated to the University in 1951 by Sir Percival David. Nearby, in Tavistock Square, the Jewish Museum has a collection of ceramics, manuscripts and embroidery.
To the east of Woburn Place, Coram's Fields is a children's park where once stood the Foundling Hospital

established in 1739 by Thomas Coram to care for destitute children. In Brunswick Square the **Thomas Coram Foundation** contains a number of relics from the original building, including paintings by Hogarth and Gainsborough, a bust of Handel by Roubiliac and a cartoon by Raphael.

In nearby Doughty Street is **Dickens' House** where the author lived with his family from 1837-39. The house is now open to the public as a museum, where exhibits include portraits, letters, manuscripts and furniture. On the top floor is an extensive display of material collected by Comte de Suzannet, including many original drawings for Dickens' novels by H.K. Browne ("Phiz").

South of Doughty Street can be seen the gardens of **Gray's Inn**, one of the four Inns of Court. A short walk down Gray's Inn Road brings you to Chancery Lane underground station.

Dickens' Portrait

DICKENS' HOUSE

Dickens' Desk

Dickens' House

EIGHTH ITINERARY

SOHO - VICTORIA EMBANKMENT - COVENT GARDEN - COURTAULD INSTITUTE - FLEET STREET - INNS OF COURT - SIR JOHN SOANE'S MUSEUM

Soho is one of London's most colourful and cosmopolitan areas, with many foreign shops and restaurants, though it also has its seamy side, and, despite the many changes over the years, it has somehow managed to retain its "village" atmosphere. The name Soho is said to derive from a 15th century hunting cry from the time when the area was still open fields. The revocation of the Edict of Nantes in 1685 led to a large number of French Huguenots arriving in London, and many of them settled in Soho. The area has continued to attract foreign communities, such as the Greeks, Italians and, more recently, the Chinese. The lively Chinese New Year celebrations in January or February are now an established tradition.

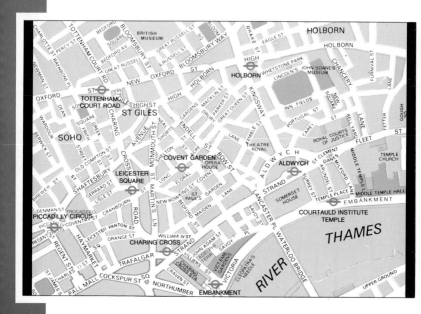

Restaurant in Soho

Over the centuries Soho has attracted prominent figures from all walks of life. Dryden, Hogarth, Canaletto, Mozart, Wagner and Marx all lived here at some time. Dr Johnson and Sir Joshua Reynolds used to meet at the Turk's Head Tavern in Gerrard Street and founded a literary club there in 1764. Soho has long-standing associations with the entertainment world, and, as well as having a number of theatres within its boundaries, has close connections with the film and music industries.

There are restaurants to suit all tastes and some of London's most characteristic pubs can be found here. Berwick Street has a lively open air market and Charing Cross Road still retains a number of secondhand bookshops.

Charing Cross Road leads south to the **Strand** which, as its name suggests, once ran alongside the Thames. It is

Soho Square

now a busy street lined by shops, theatres and hotels. South of the Strand is the **Victoria Embankment** which stretches from Westminster Bridge to Blackfriars. It was constructed between 1865-70 by Sir Joseph Bazalgette and incorporates an underground railway and a sewerage system. Moored alongside it are a number of ships, including a restaurant, a pub and the Wellington, the livery hall of the Master Mariners. By Victoria Embankment Gardens stands Cleopatra's Needle, which has nothing to do with Cleopatra but was one of a pair of obelisks which stood at Heliopolis. It was presented to Britain by Mohammed Ali and erected here in 1878, flanked by sphinxes designed by George Vulliamy.

The area between the Strand and the Thames was once occupied by the mansions of the nobility, as is indicated by street names such as York Place, Villiers Street and Arundel Street. Nothing now remains of these mansions, but the watergate of York House in Victoria Embankment Gardens shows where the Thames once

"Cleopatra's Needle" on the Victoria Embankment

reached. Adelphi Terrace reminds us of the Adam brothers' ambitious residential plans for the area in

121

A View of Victoria Embankment.

1768, called the Adelphi after the Greek word for brothers. A number of eminent people, such as Garrick the actor, lived here, but the scheme proved to be a financial disaster and now only a few Adam houses remain.

Nearby is the site of Savoy Palace, built in 1246 and later

One of the few surviving Adam Houses in the Adelphi Terrace

The Savoy Chapel, Interior

The Thames from the South Bank

the residence of John of Gaunt. It was burnt to the ground during the Peasants' Revolt of 1381 and rebuilt by Henry VII as a hospital. All that now remains is the Queen's Chapel of the Savoy, built in 1505 and restored after a fire in 1864. The Savoy Theatre was built in 1881 by Richard D'Oyly Carte to stage Gilbert and Sullivan's operettas, and was the first theatre to be lit by electricity. It was badly damaged by fire in 1990, but is undergoing restoration. Note the entrance to the Savoy Hotel, the only street in London where you must drive on the right. To the north of the Strand is **Covent Garden**, an area

Covent Garden

which was once the convent garden of Westminster Abbey. Later the land was developed by the Bedford family, and Inigo Jones designed a splendid piazza, of which St. Paul's Church on the west side is all that remains. In the 19th century the Central Market Building was added and Covent Garden was London's wholesale fruit and vegetable market until 1974, when it moved to Nine Elms, south of the river. The building has been well restored and the whole piazza has been transformed into a lively and popular area full of small shops, wine bars, restaurants and street theatre.

In the southeast corner the old Flower Market has been converted into the **London Transport Museum**, whose impressive collection of trams, buses and trains chronicles over 150 years of public transport in London. Just round the corner in Russell Street is the **Theatre Museum**. The entrance hall is suitably dramatic, with a large gilded Spirit of Gaiety and boxes from the Palace Theatre in Glasgow. Downstairs are special exhibitions and a display on the history of theatre from the 16th century to the present day.

Turning left into Bow Street you will see the **Royal Opera House**, permanent home of the Royal Opera and Ballet companies. The first theatre opened here in 1732 and the present building was designed by E.M. Barry in 1858. Opposite the theatre is Bow Street Police Station and Magistrate's Court. The first court was built here in 1748, and it was here that the novelist Henry Fielding and his brother, John, founded the famous Bow Street Runners, precursors of the Metropolitan Police. Make your way back down Bow Street and Wellington Street and you will find yourself back in the Strand. To the left the Aldwych curves past Bush House, home of the BBC World Service.

Somerset House

COURTAULD INSTITUTE GALLERIES

Diagonally opposite stands Somerset House, named after the 16th century palace built for the Lord Protector Somerset. The present Palladian building, which boasts a 600-ft facade overlooking the Thames, was designed by Sir William Chambers in 1776-86. The building houses a number of Government offices, but the north wing, which once housed the Royal Academy of Arts, is now occupied by the **Courtauld Institute Galleries**, one of London's finest art collections. The rooms themselves are worthy of attention, with some very fine ceilings, and the entrance to the galleries is up a splendid staircase. The first room contains art of the Renaissance, with two fine painted 15th century Italian chests, Botticelli's Holy

Courtauld Institute Galleries, Edouard Manet: Bar at the Folies Bergère

Trinity and Cranach's Adam and Eve. Rooms 2 and 3 contain work by Caravaggio, Lotto and Van Dyck, but are dominated by a number of fine pictures by Rubens, particularly the Descent from the Cross and the Family

Courtauld Institute Galleries, Paul Cézanne: the Card Players

of Jan Breughel. Rooms 5 and 6 hold the paintings for which the Courtauld is best known, a superb collection of Impressionist and Post-Impressionist paintings. All the major artists are represented, the best known paintings being Renoir's La Loge, Manet's Bar at the Folies-Bergère, Van Gogh's Self-Portrait with Bandaged Ear and Cézanne's The Card Players. Room 8, once the Great Room of the Royal Academy, displays Kokoschka's Prometheus Triptych high up, as intended, and has a number of thematic exhibitions. Rooms 9 and 10 are devoted to the 20th century, with works by Sickert, Sutherland, Roger Fry and Duncan Grant. Room 11

houses art of the 14th-16th centuries, including Daddi's splendid Triptych and Breughel's beautiful little Land-scape with Flight into Egypt.

In the middle of the Strand outside Somerset House stands the delightful church of St Mary-le-Strand, built by James Gibbs in 1714. The parents of Charles Dickens were married here in 1809. Further east is another "island" church, St. Clement Danes, designed by Wren in 1680-82 and restored after extensive war damage as the church of the Royal Air Force. It is most famous for its peal of bells which plays the tune "Oranges and Lemons, say the bells of St. Clement's".

The Church of St Mary-le-Strand, with the Church of St. Clement Danes in the Background

LAW COURTS

Nearby, on the north side of the Strand, are the Royal Courts of Justice, commonly known as the **Law Courts**, built to the Gothic design of G.E. Street between 1874-82. The magnificent Central Hall is 238ft. long and has a

The Law Courts, interior

mosaic pavement designed by Street. The public is admitted to the galleries during trials.

In the middle of the road is the Temple Bar Memorial, topped by a griffin, which marks the boundary between Westminster and the City of London. Beyond is Fleet Street, which takes its name from the Fleet river which

THE TEMPLE

was covered over in the 18th century and is now part of the sewers. The street was for many years known as the "Street of ink" as it was the home for most of the national newspapers, but these have recently moved to other parts of London.

Middle Temple Lane on the right leads into the **Temple**, which comprises two of the Inns of Court, Inner Temple and Middle Temple. The Inns of Court were founded in the 14th century and either train or examine all students of law before they are "called to the Bar". The Temple was originally the property of the Knights Templars, but it passed to the Crown in 1312 and was later leased to legal professors, thus initiating its legal associations. Middle Temple Hall is a splendid Elizabethan building with a magnificent hammer-beam roof. Both Inner and Middle Temple are served by Temple Church, whose circular nave of 1185 was modelled on the Church of the Holy Sepulchre in Jerusalem. On the floor of the nave

Temple Church.

are a number of fine 12th and 13th century effigies of knights.

Leave the Temple by Inner Temple Lane through a gateway over which is Prince Henry's Room, named after the eldest son of James I. It has a fine plaster ceiling and a small exhibition of Pepys memorabilia. On the other side of the street is the church of St Dunstan in the

The Interior of Middle Temple Hall

West, with a contemporary statue of Elizabeth I over the east porch. Further east is St. Bride's Church, rebuilt by Wren and restored after being badly damaged in the last war. The beautiful steeple is Wren's tallest.

In Wine Office Court to the north of Fleet Street is the Old Cheshire Cheese, an old tavern frequented, it is claimed, by Dr. Johnson. Further west, in Gough Square, is **Dr. Johnson's House**, now a museum. Johnson lived here from 1748-59 and it was here that he worked on his famous Dictionary, a copy of which is on display.

Retracing your steps westwards, turn north into Chancery Lane, where you will find the Public Record Office, the main repository of the nation's archives. In the museum can be seen the two vellum volumes of the Domesday Book, the detailed survey of England ordered by William the Conqueror in 1086.

Further up Chancery Lane on the left is Lincoln's Inn, another of the Inns of Court. It is pleasant to stroll around the precincts, though access to the buildings is restricted. Behind Lincoln's Inn are Lincoln's Inn Fields, the largest square in central London. It was laid out in 1618 by Inigo Jones, though Lindsey House on the west side is the only original building to survive. On the north side stands **Sir John Soane's Museum**, one of London's most eccentric and delightful museums. Soane, the architect of the Bank of England, lived here for the last 24 years of his life, and here are displayed, much as they were during his lifetime, his collections of antiquities, works of art and many of his architectural drawings. In the basement is the Sepulchral Chamber which houses the famous alabaster Sarcophagus of Seti I. The Picture Room on the ground floor is ingeniously fitted with hinged walls to accomodate more pictures than you would expect, just one of many surprises in this extraordinary house. Here are hung Hogarth's two famous series of paintings, The Rake's Progress and The Election.

Sir John Soane's Museum, Exterior

NINTH ITINERARY

ST. PAUL'S CATHEDRAL - OLD BAILEY - SMITHFIELD - ST. BARTHOLOMEW THE GREAT - BARBICAN - MUSEUM OF LONDON - GUILDHALL - BANK OF ENGLAND - MONUMENT - TOWER OF LONDON - TOWER BRIDGE - ST. KATHARINE DOCKS

The City of London covers an area slightly greater than a square mile, and its traditions and institutions go back many centuries. The development of mercantile trade, together with its financial and legal institutions, quite distinct from the parliamentary systems at the seat of government in Westminster, meant that successive monarchs were obliged to court rather than command it. The great craft guilds survive today in the form of the

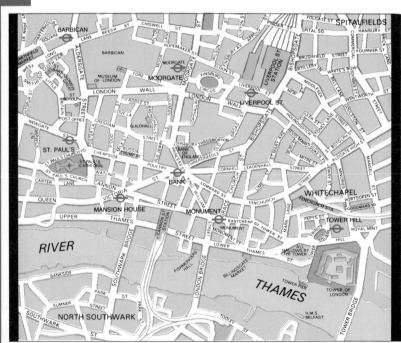

Livery Companies, which retain many ancient customs and ceremonies, including the right to elect the Lord Mayor and Sheriffs of the City of London.

In just a few days in 1666 the Great Fire devastated most of the area. Several imaginative plans were put forward to redevelop the City, but when it was rebuilt it followed the old medieval street plan. Sir Christopher Wren designed many new churches, of which 24 survived the bombs of the Second World War. Of these, his master-

St. Paul's by Night

piece is **St. Paul's Cathedral** at the top of Ludgate Hill, on a site where a Christian church has stood since the 7th century. The later church was given, in 1315, a spire nearly 500ft. high. The building was in a poor state of repair when, in 1666, it was burnt down in the Great

St. Paul's Cathedral.

Fire. In the present church, which is the seat of the Bishop of London, Wren used a clever combination of architectural styles. He originally proposed a Greek cross floorplan, but this was rejected by the Court party who, mistakenly looking forward to the country's return to Roman Catholicism, demanded the long nave necessary for its rituals and processions. Instead Wren employed a beautifully proportioned Gothic floorplan with Classical and Baroque details. The west facade has a classical look with two levels of columns topped by a pediment with a relief of the Conversion of St. Paul, and flanked by two Baroque towers. The magnificent dome is in fine classical style and technically brilliant. To support the stone lantern and cross, 365ft. above the ground, Wren constructed a concealed cone of brickwork between the outer dome of leaded timber and the inner brick dome. The inner cupola of the dome, supported by massive pillars, is painted with Sir James Thornhill's Scenes of the Life of St. Paul (1720) with mosaics of prophets and the evangelists by Salviati decorating the spandrels.

The church boasts numerous monuments to important historical figures, including the Duke of Wellington's huge equestrian monument in the North Nave Aisle and Flaxman's monument to Lord Nelson in the South Transept. In the South Choir Aisle stands the shrouded figure of John Donne (1573-1631), Dean of St. Paul's and one of England's great poets – his is one of the few monuments to survive the Great Fire and still bears scorch marks. Note also, in the South Nave Aisle, Holman Hunt's well known painting, The Light of the World. The beautifully carved choir stalls and organ case are both the work of Grinling Gibbons, and the Choir is enclosed by a fine wrought-iron screen by Jean Tijou.

The famous inscription taken from Wren's tomb can be found in the North Transept, "Si monumentum requiris circumspice" – if you seek a monument, look around you. Wren's tomb, however, lies in the Crypt, reached by the South Transept and as large as the church itself. It houses many graves and monuments, including a "Painters' Corner" commemorating Turner, Blake, Reynolds, Van Dyck, Constable and others. In the western part of the Crypt the huge marble sarcophagus made for Cardinal Wolsey in fact contains the coffin of Lord Nelson.

In the South Aisle are the stairs up to the Whispering Gallery, where the slightest sound can be heard right round its circumference. From here you get a splendid view of Thornhill's painting in the dome. The external Stone Gallery and the Golden Gallery above offer a sweeping panorama of London. Visitors may climb the last of the 627 steps to the Ball at the top of the lantern, but the view here is more limited.

To the west of St. Paul's, leading north off Ludgate Hill, runs **Old Bailey**, also the popular name for the Central Criminal Court which stands at its north end on the site of the old Newgate Prison. The court was built between 1902-7 and has a copper dome with a large figure of Justice. On certain days flowers and sweet herbs are

St. Paul's Cathedral: Interior looking up into the Dome

strewn around the courts as a reminder of the times when the stench from the prison was overpowering, and this practice brought some relief to the judges. Opposite the court is the 12th-century church of St. Sepulchre, whose bell would toll whenever an execution was carried out at Newgate.

Giltspur Street leads north into **Smithfield**, now a busy wholesale meat market, but once known as "Smooth Field", lying just outside the City walls and the setting for tournaments and fairs as well as executions. Wat Tyler, leader of the Peasants' Revolt was killed here in 1381 by the Lord Mayor, Sir William Walworth, in the presence of Richard II. On the corner of Giltspur Street stands St. Bartholomew's Hospital, founded in 1123 by Rahere, one of Henry I's courtiers. In the grounds is the church of St. Bartholomew the Less, and across the road is the entrance to **St. Bartholomew the Great**, the oldest church in London after St. John's Chapel in the Tower. This former Priory church, founded, like the hospital, by Rahere, suffered considerable damage during the Reformation, and the choir, crossing and one bay of the nave are all that survived to form the parish church as it is today. The main body of the present church is Norman in style, though it is punctuated on the south side by a 16th

St. Paul's Cathedral

century oriel window, and the Lady Chapel is 14th century.

To the north of Smithfield is Charterhouse Square, with the interesting building of the **Charterhouse** on the north side. It has been a Carthusian priory, a school and a hospital, and still has many fine buildings of the 16th century. The area to the east, across Aldersgate Street, suffered from severe bomb damage during the last war, and has now been redeveloped with many private flats and the **Barbican Centre**, opened by the Queen in 1982. The centre includes a concert hall, the home of the London Symphony Orchestra, two theatres where the Royal Shakespeare Company performs, three cinemas and an art gallery.

St. Paul's Cathedral by Night

To the south is the **Museum of London**, a splendid museum which traces the history of London and its people from prehistoric times to the present day. The galleries are arranged in chronological order, and the items on display range from paintings and costumes to reconstructed rooms and excavated objects of all sorts. The Roman section includes sculptures from the Temple of Mithras and a bikini, while the Medieval room con-

Fragment of the old Roman London Wall

tains a fine collection of pilgrim badges and a rare 15th century cradle. In the Tudor and Stuart room is the Cheapside Hoard, a superb collection of Jacobean jewellery, Samuel Pepys' chessboard and a popular reconstruction of the Great Fire. The Modern section covers Georgian, Victorian and 20th century London, and items on display include doors from Newgate Prison, an Art Deco lift from Selfridge's and the Lord Mayor's State Coach.

Walk south from the Museum of London and turn left into Gresham Street. A short way down on the left is the **Guildhall**, the home of the Corporation of the City of London and the setting for the election of the Lord Mayor and the Sheriffs, banquets and many other ceremonial events. The present building dates back to the

The Guildhall, Exterior

15th century, though it was rebuilt after being damaged in both the Great Fire and the Second World War. Nearby St. Lawrence Jewry Church is the official church of the City Corporation.

Continuing along Gresham Street and Princes Street you

come to the busy Bank intersection. To the east is the huge portico of the Royal Exchange, founded by Sir Thomas Gresham in 1565 and the third building on the site. It is now occupied by the London International

The Guildhall, Interior with the Ceremony of the Election of the Sheriffs of the City of London

Financial Futures Exchange. On the north side is the **Bank of England**, popularly known ad the "Old Lady of Threadneedle Street". The building is the work of Sir John Soane, though there have been many modifications. In Bartholomew Lane is the entrance to the **Bank of England Museum**, which tells the story of the Bank from when it was granted the Royal Charter in 1694 to the world of modern banking. To the east is the modern Stock Exchange, which has a visitors' gallery, though there is little activity on the floor in today's world of computers. On the south side is the **Mansion House**, the official residence of the Lord Mayor. A short detour eastwards along Cornhill and Leadenhall Street will bring you to the striking modern building of Lloyd's designed by Richard Rogers.

From Bank, a walk down King William Street brings you to the **Monument**, a 202ft. column designed by Wren to commemorate the Great Fire, which broke out to the east at a baker's shop in Pudding Lane. A walk up its 311 steps will give you an impressive view of the surrounding area. Monument Street leads into Lower Thames Street, where, to the west, is the fine spire of Wren's St. Magnus the Martyr. Further east is the building of the former Billingsgate Market, now redeveloped, but once the main fish market.

The Church of **All Hallows by the Tower** in Byward Street was founded in the 7th century and was rebuilt after being damaged in the Second World War. It still retains a number of elements of the earlier building,

Museum of London

including a Saxon arch, a 14th century crypt with a Roman pavement and a font cover carved by Grinling Gibbons. William Penn was baptised in the church and it was from the tower that Pepys watched the progress of

The Bank of England

The Royal Exchange

The Tower of London, the Tower Bridge.
Tower of London. The White Tower

Aerial View of Tower Bridge.

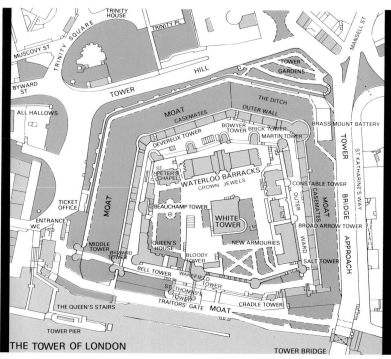

THE TOWER OF LONDON

152

the Great Fire in 1666. In Trinity Square Gardens is a plaque marking the spot of the scaffold where, during the 14th-18th centuries no fewer than 75 traitors were executed.

The Tower of London covers an area of 18 acres and is guarded by the Yeoman Warders, popularly called "Beefeaters", who also offer guided tours, clad in their traditional Tudor uniforms. The Tower has, down the centuries, served as citadel, palace, prison and menagerie, and has been closely associated with many important events in England's history.

The Tower of London: a Beefeater

Passing through the Middle Tower you cross the moat and pass under the Byward Tower. Ahead of you is the 13th century Bell Tower where, among others, Sir Thomas More, Princess Elizabeth and the Duke of Monmouth were imprisoned. A little further on to the right is Traitors' Gate, which served as the entrance for prisoners brought by river, including Anne Boleyn and Princess Elizabeth. Opposite is the Bloody Tower, so-called because of its association with the murder of the "Princes in the Tower" in 1483. Other notable inmates were Sir Walter Raleigh, who lived here with his family, Archbishop Laud and the infamous Judge Jeffreys.

Tower of London: the Chapel of St. John

Wakefield Tower, to the right, is where Henry VI was murdered in 1471. Passing through the archway in the Bloody Tower you come to the Inner Ward, dominated by the White Tower, the original keep started in 1078 for William I by Gundulf, Bishop of Rochester. It got its name from the white Caen stone, but if was later whitewashed to maintain its colour. Sir Christopher Wren was later responsible for the external restoration, when he added the cupolas at the four corners and replaced most of the original windows. In 1674 some bones, presumed to be those of the murdered "Little Princes", were found under an external staircase in the south wall. The White Tower now contains a superb collection of arms and armour, arranged over several floors. On the second floor is the beautiful Chapel of St. John, the oldest church in London, dating from 1080.

Tower of London: Crown Jewels

To the west of the White Tower is Tower Green where you will see the famous ravens. It is said that if they leave the Tower, the Kingdom will fall. A brass plate to the north marks the site of the executioner's block where many royal or noble persons were beheaded, including Anne Boleyn, Katherine Howard and Lady Jane Grey.

9

On the west side of the Green is Beauchamp Tower, whose walls are covered in inscriptions carved by prisoners. To the north is the Chapel of St. Peter ad Vincula, where many of those who died in the Tower were buried.

To the north of the White Tower are the Waterloo Barracks, where the Crown Jewels are displayed. Most of the regalia was dispersed during the Commonwealth, so most of the present collection dates from after the Restoration. The oldest crown is St. Edward's Crown and the oldest piece in the regalia is the Spoon used at the coronation of King John in 1199.

To the south of the White Tower is a History Gallery illustrating the history of the Tower, and near here it is possibile to take a walk round the top of the Inner Curtain Wall. In the Lower Martin Tower is an exhibition of torture and punishment, explaining how the instruments were used. By applying in advance, it is possible to attend the daily Ceremony of the Keys, which

Tower Bridge

is held at 10 pm when the Tower is formally closed for the night.

Crossing the Thames to the west is **Tower Bridge**, with its twin towers and massive bascules which are still raised occasionally to allow the passage of tall ships. It was built from 1886-94 to the plans of Sir Horace Jones and Sir John Wolfe Barry, and was designed in such a way as to blend with the Tower of London. The bridge is now open to the public, and there are exhibitions on its history as well as superb views from the walkway. On the south side of the bridge is a small museum housing the original steam engines once used to raise the bascules.

To the east of Tower Bridge on the north side are the **St. Katharine Docks**, constructed in 1827 by Thomas Telford but now converted into a yacht marina and leisure centre. It is an attractive area to wander in, with shops, restaurants, a hotel and the Dickens Inn pub. There are also a number of interesting boats moored here, including Thames sailing barges.

Tower Bridge at Sunset.

TENTH ITINERARY

IMPERIAL WAR MUSEUM - LAMBETH PA-LACE - SOUTH BANK CENTRE - MUSEUM OF THE MOVING IMAGE - SOUTHWARK CATHEDRAL - LONDON BRIDGE - GREEN-WICH - THAMES BARRIER

A short walk from Lambeth North underground station is the **Imperial War Museum**, housed in part of the old Bethlem Royal Hospital for the Insane, more commonly called "Bedlam". The museum records all British and Commonwealth military activity since 1914 by means of vehicles, weapons and other relics, as well as a superb collection of paintings, photographs and documents. There are regular special exhibitions and new developments are the Blitz and Trench Experiences which come with the sights and sounds of the real thing.

Turning left outside the museum continue down Lambeth Road. At the end on the right is the old parish

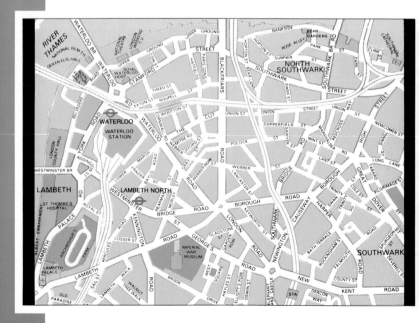

The Imperial War Museum

Lambeth Palace, the Gatehouse

church of St. Mary-at-Lambeth. It has been restored and now houses a small **Museum of Garden History**, run by the Tradescant Trust. The churchyard contains the unusual tomb of John Tradescant and his son, both of whom were influential gardeners and lived in Lambeth in the 17th century. Also buried here is Admiral Bligh of the "Bounty", another local resident.

Next to the church is **Lambeth Palace**, which has been the London residence of the Archbishops of Canterbury since 1207. The impressive red brick gatehouse is called Morton's Tower after Cardinal Morton, who had it built in 1495. The Great Hall is medieval in origin, but was

The South Bank Arts Complex

restored in the 17th century and again after the last war. It contains a valuable library of illustrated manuscripts and early printed books. The Guard Chamber has an unusual 14th century timber roof and houses a fine collection of portraits of archbishops by such important artists as Holbein, Van Dyck, Hogarth and Reynolds. The 15th century Lollards' Tower is named after the followers of Wyclif, the reformer, who are supposed to have been imprisoned here. Wyclif himself was tried in the Chapel in 1378. The Crypt, beneath the Chapel, is the oldest part of the building.

After enjoying the view across the Thames towards the

Houses of Parliament, continue north to St. Thomas' Hospital, which was founded in 1173 in Southwark but moved here in 1868. Housed in part of the hospital is the **Florence Nightingale Museum** which illustrates the life and times of Florence Nightingale and her contribution to medical science. On display are a number of her possessions, including a lamp from the Crimean War.

On the other side of Westminster Bridge is County Hall, an impressive building which was the home of the Greater London Council until its abolition in 1986. Beyond Jubilee Gardens is the **South Bank Centre** on the site of the 1951 Festival of Britain. The Royal Festival Hall, London's major concert hall, has excellent acoustics and houses a splendid organ. Next door are two smaller concert halls, the Queen Elizabeth Hall and Purcell Room. The Hayward Gallery opened in 1968 and holds regular art exhibitions. Also here is the National Film Theatre which, as well as four cinemas, has a popular restaurant overlooking the Thames.

The newest part of the complex is the award-winning **Museum of the Moving Image**, which is housed under the south end of Waterloo Bridge. This well-designed and exciting museum tells the story of cinema and television by means of interactive exhibits, reconstructions and actor-guides. There are plenty of historic exhibits and film extracts, and you can "read the news" and "fly" like Superman.

Beyond Waterloo Bridge is the **Royal National Theatre**, which was designed by Denys Lasdun and opened in 1976. Within the complex are three theatres, the open stage Olivier, the more conventional Lyttleton and the smaller, experimental, Cottesloe. Musical events and exhibitions are held in the foyer, where there are several good places to eat.

A short walk along Upper Ground takes you past Gabriel's Wharf, an open air market, to Blackfriars Bridge. Steps take you down to the riverside walk, which offers splendid views of St. Paul's and the City. Further along, in Cardinal Cap Alley, are some 18th century houses in one of which Sir Christopher Wren is said to have lived while he built St. Paul's. The area beyond this is where, in the 16th and 17th centuries, London's theatres developed, and there was much excitement in 1989 when the remains of the Rose and the Globe theatres were found. The Rose will be on view in the new development planned for the site in Park Street. In Bear Gardens is the Shakespeare Globe Museum which houses an exhi-

Southwark Cathedral.

SOUTHWARK CATHEDRAL

bition on Elizabethan and Jacobean theatre. Nearby, as part of the International Shakespeare Globe Centre, a reproduction of the Globe Theatre is being built.

Beyond Southwark Bridge you will find the attractive Anchor Inn, dating from the 15th century but rebuilt in the 18th century. In Clink Street are some remains of Winchester Palace, the residence of the Bishops of Winchester who, until the 17th century, controlled the Liberty of the Clink here which, being outside the jurisdiction of the City, became the entertainment centre of London, with theatres, bear gardens and brothels. The bishops also controlled the Clink Prison which gave its name to prisons in general. In St. Mary Overy Dock is the Kathleen & May, a schooner built in 1900 and which now contains a small exhibition.

Southwark Cathedral or, more correctly the Cathedral and Collegiate Church of St. Saviour and St. Mary Overie, is a fine Gothic church, erected on the site of a nunnery which later became an Augustinian priory. The present church was begun in 1106 and the choir and retro-choir remain from the rebuilding of 1207. The tower dates from the 13th and 15th centuries, but the nave had to be rebuilt in the 19th century, having fallen into disrepair. At the west end of the north aisle are some interesting carved bosses from the 15th century roof and further east is the decorated tomb of John Gower, poet and friend of Chaucer. Shakespeare is commemorated by a memorial in the south aisle and a stained glass window depicting characters from his plays. The choir contains a much restored altar screen of 1520 and the choir aisles house some fine tombs. The Harvard Chapel, to the east of the north transept, is dedicated to the memory of John Harvard, founder of Harvard University, who was born in the parish and baptised in the church. At the east end of the church is the beautiful retro-choir, with its four aisles separated by graceful columns.

To the south is Borough High Street which has for centuries been the main route to the south east. It was also the starting point for pilgrimages to the shrine of St. Thomas à Becket at Canterbury and was lined with inns and hostelries. The most famous was the Tabard Inn

LONDON BRIDGE

17th century View of London

mentioned in Chaucer's Canterbury Tales, now long
gone. The George Inn is the last surviving galleried inn
in London and is now owned by the National Trust.

To the north is **London Bridge**. There has been a bridge
here since the wooden bridge erected in the first century
and until 1729 London Bridge was the only Thames
crossing. In 1176 Henry II commissioned a new bridge of
stone from Peter of Colechurch. This was soon lined
with houses and there was a chapel to St. Thomas à
Becket in the middle. At each end was a fortified gateway and on the spikes heads of traitors were displayed as
a deterrent to others. A new bridge was designed in 1825
by John Rennie, but this was sold in 1970 to Lake Hav-
asu City in Arizona and replaced by the present bridge,
built between 1967-73.

From the southern end of the bridge go east down Duke
Street Hill which leads into Tooley Street. Here, on the
right, is the **London Dungeon**, an exhibition, suitably
located under damp railway arches, which illustrates
some of the more unpleasant aspects of Britain's history.
To the north of Tooley Street is a new development
called London Bridge City which mixes modern buildings with some attractively converted warehouses.

10

There is a pleasant riverside walk starting at London Bridge offering interesting views. A little way along is Hay's Galleria which has been imaginatively rebuilt from an old warehouse. The complex contains a number of shops and restaurants and a curious sculpture called Navigators. Further east is moored the **HMS Belfast**, a Royal Navy cruiser built in 1938 and now serving as a museum, run by the Imperial War Museum. Beyond Tower Bridge is the attractive Anchor Brewery, now converted into apartments. A little way along the river-front is Butler's Wharf, which houses the **Design**

Greenwich

Museum, opened in 1989 to study and illustrate the contribution of design in everyday life, with regular special exhibitions.

There are several ways to travel to **Greenwich**. One of the most pleasant and interesting is by boat from Westminster, Charing Cross or Tower Pier. You can also go from Tower Gateway on the Docklands Light Railway, which takes you to Island Gardens on the Isle of Dogs, leaving a short walk under the Thames. Either way you

Royal Naval College: the Painted Hall.

get a good view of the great changes taking place in what was until recently a rather neglected area of London, the **Docklands**. Vast areas of London's East End are being commercially redeveloped with a fascinating, though not always pleasing, mixture of modern architecture and converted buildings. The most visible development is at Canary Wharf on the Isle of Dogs, which includes the tallest building in Britain.

Moored to Greenwich Pier is the **Cutty Sark**, the last of the sea clippers, built in 1869. On board is an excellent collection of ships' figureheads and an exhibition on the ship's history. Berthed nearby is Gipsy Moth IV in which

Greenwich: the Queen's House

Sir Francis Chichester circumnavigated the world single-handed in 1966-67.

The **Royal Naval College** stands on the site of Placentia, a favourite palace of the Tudor monarchs. The present building was designed by Sir Christopher Wren as Greenwich Hospital, but was taken over by the College in 1873. Open to the public are the Chapel and the Painted Hall, so-called because of the superb wall and ceiling paintings by Sir James Thornhill.

Behind the College is the **National Maritime Museum** which houses an extensive collection illustrating Britain's maritime heritage, with many artifacts and relics from the Tudor period onwards, including the uniform worn by Nelson at the Battle of Trafalgar. In the centre is the Queen's House, designed in Palladian style by Inigo Jones and built from 1616-35 for the queens of James I and Charles I. It has recently been restored and is notable for its collection of maritime paintings. The two wings were added early in the 19th century to house the Royal Hospital School, but this moved to Suffolk in 1933 and the museum opened here in 1937.

Behind the museum is Greenwich Park, laid out by Le Nôtre for Charles II. On a hill stands the **Old Royal Observatory**, built in 1675 and now part of the National Maritime Museum. Flamsteed House was built by Wren for Flamsteed, the first Astronomer Royal, and now contains displays on navigation and astronomy. In front of the observatory a line marks the zero meridian of longitude from which time relative to Greenwich Mean Time is calculated. Nearby is a statue of General Wolfe, and by the west gate of the park is Macartney House where he lived. Just outside the park, in Chesterfield Walk, is Ranger's House, a handsome late 17th century redbrick mansion. It houses the Suffolk Collection of Tudor and Jacobean portraits and the Dolmetsch collection of musical instruments.

A short distance downstream of Greenwich, and accessible by road or river, is the **Thames Barrier**, a magnificent feat of engineering, completed in 1983 to protect London from potentially disastrous flooding. Spanning the full width of the Thames, it consists of ten separate steel gates, making it the largest moveable flood barrier in the world. When raised, the four main gates stand as high as a five-storey building and are as wide as the opening of Tower Bridge. On the south side of the river is the Thames Barrier Centre, which houses an exhibition explaining how the barrier works.

Thames Barrier.

ELEVENTH ITINERARY

HAMPSTEAD - HIGHGATE - DULWICH - CHISWICK - KEW - RICHMOND - HAMPTON COURT - WINDSOR

This final chapter is not really an itinerary, but is a selection of some of the more interesting attractions to be found outside the centre of London.

To the north is **Hampstead**, which has many attractive old houses, particularly in Church Row. In Keats Grove is **Keats House**, home to the poet from 1818-20 and now a museum. In Maresfield Gardens is the house where Sigmund Freud spent the last year of his life, now the **Freud Museum**, housing his library, his collection of antiquities and the famous couch. Nearby is Hampstead Heath, which offers fine walking and splendid views

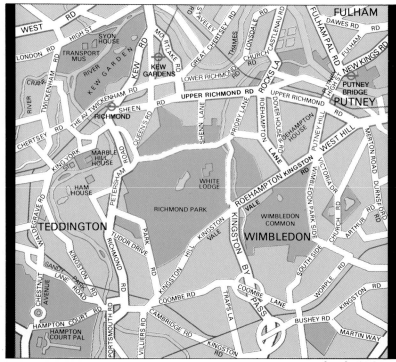

over London. On the north side of the Heath is **Kenwood House**, set in its own wooded grounds. Robert Adam rebuilt the house in 1764 for the Earl of Mansfield, and the Library, with ceiling paintings by Zucchi, is one of his finest rooms. The house contains a fine collection of paintings, including works by Gainsborough, Reynolds, Turner, Vermeer and Rembrandt.

In nearby Highgate is the famous **Highgate Cemetery**, founded in 1838 and best known for the tomb of Karl Marx in the eastern part. The western part is the more interesting, with many fascinating tombs and catacombs. Buried here are the scientist, Michael Faraday and Christina Rossetti, the poet.

Dulwich, in the south of London, retains some of the

The Horniman Museum

charm of the village it once was and contains a number of good Georgian houses. It is perhaps best known for the public school, Dulwich College, but is also home to the oldest public art gallery in Britain, **Dulwich Picture Gallery**. The gallery was designed by Sir John Soane and opened to the public in 1817. The gallery has a particularly fine collection of Dutch paintings, including works by Rembrandt, Ruisdael, Hobbema and Cuyp. There are a number of 17th and 18th century portraits by British artists such as Lely, Hogarth and Gainsborough, and others artists represented include Raphael, Canaletto, Rubens, Murillo and Poussin.

A short distance away is the **Horniman Museum**, designed in Art Nouveau style by C. Harrison Townsend. It houses a collection started by Frederich J. Horniman, the tea merchant, and includes a fine ethnographic collection and a display of musical instruments. Chiswick, in west London, was a fashionable area in the 17th and 18th centuries, and still retains some delightful period houses along Chiswick Mall. **Chiswick House** was designed by the 3rd Earl of Burlington in 1729 as a "temple to the arts" and is based on Palladio's Villa Capra near Vicenza. The interior was designed by William Kent, and there are some fine ceilings and chimney

Chiswick House

pieces, as well as paintings by Kneller and Reni. Kent also designed the gardens, which contain a number of classical statues and temples. In nearby Hogarth Lane is **Hogarth's House**, the summer residence of the great 18th century artist from 1749 until his death in 1764. It houses a collection of prints of his paintings.

West of Chiswick, but on the south side of the Thames, are the famous Royal Botanic Gardens, better known as **Kew Gardens**. The first botanic garden here was laid out in 1759 and covered nine acres, but they now cover an area of about 300 acres. The gardens are worth a visit at any time of year, but are particularly attractive in the spring and the autumn. Just inside the main gate is Kew

Kew Gardens: Kew Palace

Palace, built in 1631, whose formal garden is well worth a visit. The elegant Orangery nearby was designed by Sir William Chambers in 1761 and now houses a shop and tearoom. To the south is the splendid new Princess of Wales Conservatory, which uses modern technology to provide ten different tropical environments. Nearby is the pond, overlooked by Decimus Burton's famous Palm House, built in 1848 of iron and glass. Further

Kew Gardens. The Palm House.

south is the Temperate House, also designed by Burton, and beyond is Chambers' famous pagoda. To the west is Queen Charlotte's Cottage, built in 1772 as a royal summer house. It is set among woods that are carpeted in bluebells in the spring.

Kew Gardens: the Palm House

Kew Gardens: Temple

South of Kew is **Richmond Park**, 2500 acres of sylvan countryside, enclosed in 1637 by Charles I as a royal hunting reserve, and now home to red and fallow deer. The village of Petersham borders the western edge of the park and nearby is **Ham House** which dates from 1610. It has some superb 17th century furnishings and a fine carved staircase. It also houses a number of portraits, including a Hilliard miniature of Elizabeth I.

Kew Gardens: Queen's Cottage

HAMPTON COURT

A few miles to the south, and splendidly situated by the Thames, is **Hampton Court Palace**. It was begun in 1514 by Cardinal Wolsey, but was appropriated by Henry VIII when the great churchman fell from favour. Henry

Hampton Court Palace

added the Chapel and the Great Hall, with its fine hammerbeam roof. Two centuries later Sir Christopher Wren built the south and east wings for William III. The entrance to the palace is through the Great Gatehouse, in front of which is a battlemented bridge guarded by the

HAMPTON COURT

The East Front, with the Broad Walk and the Great Fountain

The Fountain Court

HAMPTON COURT

The Clock Court

"King's Beasts". Cross Base Court and pass through Anne Boleyn's Gateway into Clock Court, named after the astronomical clock made for Henry VIII. From here the State Apartments are reached via the King's Staircase. These rooms contain some fine period furniture and there are some splendid decorated ceilings, including several by Verrio. Also on display is an extensive collection of paintings from the Royal Collection, including many Italian and Dutch works of note and a number of portraits by Kneller and Lely.

The formal gardens to the east of the palace were laid out for William III, and to the south are a number of smaller gardens, including the delightful Pond Garden laid out by Henry VIII. Also here is the Great Vine, planted in

Windsor Castle. The Long Walk.

1768 and still producing a good annual crop of grapes. In the Lower Orangery are the famous Mantegna paintings, the Triumph of Julius Caesar, bought by Charles I in 1629. To the north of the palace is the popular maze, which was planted here during the reign of William III. 21 miles west of the centre of London, on the south bank of the Thames, is the small town of Windsor, dominated by the imposing edifice of **Windsor Castle**. The first, wooden, castle was built in 1066 by William I, and over the centuries many monarchs have rebuilt and added to it. It is still used as a royal residence, so that access to parts of the castle may be restricted. After passing through Henry VIII's Gateway you will see ahead of you the magnificent St. George's Chapel, built between 1478-1511 in Perpendicular style. It is the shrine of the Order of the Garter, and the crests and banners of the Knights can be seen above the stalls. The impressive Garter Ceremony takes place each year in June. Ten

Windsor Castle. King Henry VIII Gate.

Windsor Castle. The Garter Procession.

sovereigns are buried in the chapel – Henry VIII is buried in a tomb under the Choir next to Jane Seymour, the mother of his only male heir. Another chapel to the east, built by Henry III, was converted by Queen Victoria into the Albert Memorial Chapel, in memory of her beloved husband. Past the impressive Round Tower are the State Apartments, which contain fine furniture and paintings from the Royal Collection. Also worth a visit is Queen Mary's Dolls' House, designed by Lutyens and presented to the nation in 1923 by Queen Mary. Opposite the castle is Windsor & Eton Central Station, which has been converted into the Royalty & Empire exhibition, recreating the pageantry of Queen Victoria's Diamond Jubilee.

Crossing Windsor Bridge you come to Eton, with many attractive period houses in its main street. It is, of course, best known for its public school, **Eton College**, which was founded in 1440 by Henry VI. At certain times it is possible to visit some of the historic parts of the school.

TOURIST INFORMATION CENTRES

The London Tourist Board runs a number of Tourist Information Centres. These can be found at the following locations.

Victoria Station Forecourt, SW1. Mon-Sat 0800-1900, Sun 0800-1700.

Extended summer hours. Services include hotel booking service, theatre and sightseeing tour reservations, bookshop.

Harrods, Knightsbridge (basement). Open store hours.

Selfridges, Oxford Street (basement). Open store hours.

Liverpool Street Station, EC2. Mon-Fri 0930-1830. Sat 0830-1830. Sun 0830-1530.

Heathrow Terminals 1,2,3 Underground Station. Daily 0800-1830.

Telephone Information Service 071-730 3488. Mon-Fri 0900-1800.

LONDON TRANSPORT TRAVEL INFORMATION CENTRES

For travel information telephone 071-222 1234 (24-hours) or visit one of the following Travel Information Centres:
Euston Station
Kings Cross Station
Piccadilly Circus Station
Heathrow Airport
Oxford Circus Station
Victoria Station

BRITISH RAIL TRAVEL CENTRES

For information on travel by rail outside London, visit one of the following centres.
Heathrow Airport
Kings Cross Station
Waterloo Station
Paddington Station
Gatwick Airport
12 Regent Street, SW1 (British Travel Centre)
14 Kingsgate Parade, Victoria Street, SW1
87 King William Street EC4
Cannon Street Station
Liverpool Street Station
Euston Station
St. Pancras Station

OPENING HOURS OF MUSEUMS GALLERIES & MONUMENTS

KEY: NYD New Year's Day   GF Good Friday   ES Easter Sunday   EM Easter Monday   MD May Day Holiday   CE Christmas Eve   CD Christmas Day   BD Boxing Day   BH Bank Holidays (including all above days). £ Admission charge. Numbers in brackets refer to the itinerary each attraction is described in.

Apsley House (Wellington Museum) (4) Tues-Sun 1100-1700. Closed Mondays (except BH), GF, MD, CE, CD, BD, NYD. £

Bank of England Museum (9) Mon-Fri 1000-1700. From GF to September additionally Sat, Sun and BH. Closed CD, BD, NYD.

Banqueting House (2) Tues-Sat 1000-1700. Sun 1400-1700. Closed CE, CD, BD, NYD, GF and at short notice for government functions. £

Barbican Centre (9) Mon-Sat 0900-2300. Sun and BH 1200-2300. Closed CE, CD.

British Museum & British Library (7) Mon-Sat 1000-1700. Sun 1430-1800. Closed CE, CD, BD, NYD, GF, MD.

Cabinet War Rooms (2) Daily 1000-1800. Closed CE, CD, BD, NYD. £

Carlyle's House (5) Easter-Oct Wed-Sun & BH 1100-1700. £

Chelsea Physic Garden (5) Mid-March-mid-Oct Sun & Wed 1400-1700. (During Chelsea Flower Show Daily 1200-1700). £

Chiswick House (11) Easter-Sept Daily 1000-1800. Oct-Easter Daily 1000-1600. Closed CE, CD, BD, NYD. £

Commonwealth Institute (5) Mon-Sat 1000-1700 Sun 1400-1700. Closed CD, BD, NYD, GF, MD.

Courtauld Institute Galleries (8) Mon-Sat 1000-1800 Sun 1400-1800. Closed CD, BD, NYD, GF, Easter Sat, ES, EM, BH. £

Crosby Hall (5) Daily 1000-1200 & 1415-1700. Closed CD.

Cutty Sark (10) Mon-Sat 1000-1730 Sun 1200-1730 (closes 1630 in winter). Closed CE, CD, BD. £

Design Museum (10) Tues-Sun & BH 1130-1800. Closed CE, CD, BD, December 27, NYD. £

Dickens' House (7) Mon-Sat 1000-1730. Closed BH. £

Dr Johnson's House (8) Mon-Sat 1100-1730 (Closes 1700 Oct-April). Closed BH, CE. £

Dulwich Picture Gallery (11) Tues-Fri 1000-1300 & 1400-1700 Sat 1100-1700 Sun 1400-1700. Closed CE, CD, BD, GF, ES. £

Florence Nightingale Museum (10) Tues-Sun & BH 1000-1600. Closed CD, BD, NYD, GF, ES. £

Freud Museum (11) Wed-Sun 1200-1700. Phone 071-435 2002 for BH opening hours. £

Guards Museum (3) Sat-Thurs 1000-1600. Closed CD, NYD and some ceremonial days. £

Guildhall (9) May-Sept Daily 1000-1700 Oct-April Mon-Sat 1000-1700. Closed CD, BD, NYD, GF, EM and for civic functions.

Guinness World of Records (4) Daily 1000-2200. Closed CD. £

Ham House (11) April-Sept Daily 1100-1730. Closed CE, CD, BD, NYD, GF, MD. £

Hampton Court Palace (11) Mid-March – mid-Oct Daily 0930-1800 Mid-Oct–mid-March Daily 0930-1630. Closed CE, CD, BD, NYD. £

Hayward Gallery (10) Thurs-Mon 1000-1800 Tues-Wed 1000-2000. Closed CE, CD, BD, NYD, GF, MD & between exhibitions. £

Highgate Cemetery (11)
East Side – Daily 1000-1600 (April-Oct 1700)
West Side – Sat & Sun tours on the hour 1000-1600 Mon-Fri tours 1200, 1400 & 1500. £

HMS Belfast (10) March-Oct Daily 1000-1720 Nov-March Daily 1000-1600. Closed CE, CD, BD, NYD. £

Hogarth's House (11) Mon & Wed-Sat 1100-1800 Sun 1400-1800 (Oct-March closes 1600). Closed first 2 weeks in Sept & last 3 weeks December, NYD, GF.

Horniman Museum (11) Mon-Sat 1030-1800 Sun 1400-1800. Closed CE, CD, BD.

Houses of Parliament & Westminster Hall (1) may only be visited by special arrangement with a Member of Parliament, though you may attend a debate by queueing at St. Stephen's Entrance.

Imperial War Museum (10) Daily 1000-1800. Closed CE, CD, BD, NYD. £

Institute of Contemporary Arts (3) Daily 1200-2300. Closed BH. £

Jewel Tower (1) Easter-Sept Daily 1000-1800 Oct-Easter Tues-Sun 1000-1600. Closed CE, CD, BD, NYD. £

Jewish Museum (7) April-Sept Tues-Fri & Sun 1000-1600 Oct-March Tues-Thurs & Sun 1000-1600 Fri 1000-1245. Closed BH & Jewish festivals.

Keats' House (11) April-Oct Mon-Fri 1400-1800 Sat 1000-1300 & 1400-1700 Sun & BH 1400-1700 Nov-March Mon-Fri 1300-1700 Sat 1000-1300 & 1400-1700 Sun 1400-1700. Closed CE, CD, BD, NYD, GF, ES, MD.

Kensington Palace (5) Mon-Sat 0900-1700 Sun 1300-1700. Closed CE, CD, BD, NYD, GF. £

Kenwood House (11) Easter-Sept Daily 1000-1800 Oct-Easter Daily 1000-1600. Closed CE, CD, BD, NYD.

Kew Gardens (11) Daily 0930-Dusk. Closed CD, NYD. £

Kew Palace (11) Easter-September Daily 1100-1730. £

Lambeth Palace (10) Group tours by appointment only.

Leighton House (5) Mon-Sat 1100-1700. Closed BH.

Linley Sambourne House (5) March-Oct Wed 1000-1600 Sun 1400-1700. £

London Dungeon (10) April-Sept Daily 1000-1730 Oct-March Daily 1000-1630. Closed CE, CD, BD. £

London Planetarium (6) Programmes daily from 1220 (1020 Sat & Sun) 1700. Closed CD. £

London Transport Museum (8) Daily 1000-1800. Closed CE, CD, BD. £

London Zoo (6) March-Oct Daily 0900-1800 or dusk. Nov-Feb Daily 1000-1600. Closed CD. £

Madame Tussauds (6) Daily 1000-1730. Closed CD. £

Monument (9) April-Sept Mon-Fri 0900-1800 Sat & Sun 1400-1800. Oct-March Mon-Sat 0900-1600. £

Museum of London (9) Tues-Sat 1000-1800 Sun 1400-1800. Closed Mondays (except BH), CD, BD.

Museum of Mankind (4) Mon-Sat 1000-1700 Sun 1430-1800. Closed CE, CD, BD, NYD, GF, MD.

Museum of Garden History (10) March-early December Mon-Fri 1100-1500 Sun 1030-1700.

Museum of the Moving Image (10) Tues-Sat 1000-2000 Sun & BH 1000-1800 (June-Sept 2000). Closed CE, CD, BD. £

National Army Museum (5) Mon-Sat 1000-1730 Sun 1400-1730. Closed CE, CD, BD, GF, MD.

National Gallery (2) Mon-Sat 1000-1800 Sun 1400-1800 (June, July & Sept open Wed until 2000). Closed CE, CD, BD, NYD, GF, MD.

National Maritime Museum (10) Mon-Sat 1000-1800 (1700 in winter) Sun 1400-1800 (1700 in winter). Closed CE, CD, BD, NYD, GF, MD. £

National Portrait Gallery (2) Mon-Fri 1000-1700 Sat 1000-1800 Sun 1400-1800. Closed CE, CD, BD, NYD, GF, MD.

National Postal Museum (9) Mon-Thurs 0930-1630 Fri 0930-1600. Closed weekends and BH.

Natural History Museum (5) Mon-Sat 1000-1800 Sun 1100-1800. Closed CE, CD, BD, NYD, GF. £

Percival David Foundation of Chinese Art (7) Mon-Fri 1030-1700. Closed weekends and BH.

Pollock's Toy Museum (6) Mon-Sat 1000-1700. Closed BH.

Prince Henry's Room (8) Mon-Fri 1345-1700. Closed BH.

Queen's Gallery (3) Tues-Sat 1030-1700 Sun 1400-1700. Closed Mondays (except BH) and between exhibitions. £

Ranger's House (10) Easter-Sept Daily 1000-1800 Oct-Easter Daily 1000-1600. Closed CE, CD, BD, NYD.

Rock Circus (4) Daily 1100-2100. Closed CD. £

Royal Academy of Arts (4) Daily 1000-1800. Closed CD. £

Royal Hospital Chelsea (5) Mon-Fri 1000-1200 & 1400-1600 Sun from April-Sept 1400-1600. Closed CD, GF.

Royal Mews (3) Oct-March Wed 1200-1600 April-July Wed & Thurs 1200-1600 July-Sept Wed-Fri 1200-1600. Closed BH & Royal Ascot week. £

Royal Naval College (10) Fri-Wed 1430-1700. Closed CE, CD, GF and occasionally for operational requirements.

St. Paul's Cathedral (9) Mon-Sat 0800-1800. Ambulatory, Galleries & Crypt Mon-Fri 1000-1615 Sat 1100-1615 (£ Ambulatory, Galleries & Crypt).

Science Museum (5) Mon-Sat 1000-1800 Sun 1100-1800. Closed CD, NYD. £

Sir John Soane's Museum (8) Tues-Sat 1000-1700. Closed BH.

Southwark Cathedral (10) Daily 0800-1800.

Tate Gallery (1) Mon-Sat 1000-1750 Sun 1400-1750. Closed CE, CD, BD, NYD, GF, MD.

Temple Church (8) Daily 1000-1600. Closed some days in Aug & Sept.

Thames Barrier Visitor Centre (10) Mon-Fri 1030-1700 Sat & Sun 1030-1730. Closed CD, BD, NYD. £

Theatre Museum (8) Tues-Sun 1100-1900. Closed CD. £

Thomas Coram Foundation (7) Mon-Fri 1000-1600. Closed BH and when used for conferences. Phone 071-278 2424 to check.

Tower Bridge (9) April-Oct Daily 1000-1830 Nov-March Daily 1000-1645. Closed CE, CD, BD, NYD, GF. £

Tower of London (9) March-Oct Mon-Sat 0930-1700 Sun 1400-1700 Nov-Feb Mon-Sat 0930-1600. Closed CE, CD, BD, NYD, GF, Jewel House closed part of January & February. £

Victoria & Albert Museum (5) Mon-Sat 1000-1800 Sun 1430-1800. Closed CE, CD, BD, NYD, GF, MD. £ (Voluntary donation).

Wallace Collection (6) Mon-Sat 1000-1700 Sun 1400-1700. Closed CE, CD, BD, NYD, GF, MD.

Westminster Abbey (1)
Nave & Cloisters Daily 0800-1800 (1945 Wed)
Royal Chapels Mon-Fri 0900-1645 Sat 0900-1445 & 1545-1745
Chapter House & Museum Daily 1030-1600
£ to Royal Chapels, Chapter House & Museum.

Windsor Castle (11) Precincts open daily from 1000 except Garter Day (third Monday of June).
St. George's Chapel Mon-Sat 1045-1545 Sun 1400-1545. Closed CE, CD.
State Apartments Mon-Sat 1030-1600 Sun 1230-1600. Closed April, June, December & GF. £
Opening times may vary. Telephone (0753) 831118 to check.

THE LONDON UNDERGROUND

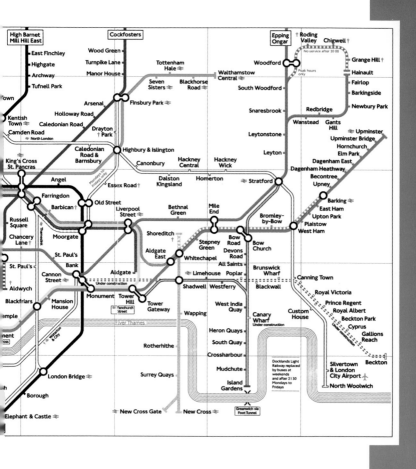

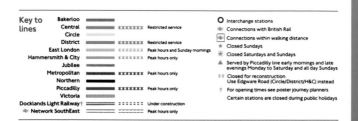

Key to lines

Bakerloo	
Central	▨▨▨▨▨ Restricted service
Circle	
District	▨▨▨▨▨ Restricted service
East London	▨▨▨▨▨ Peak hours and Sunday mornings
Hammersmith & City	▨▨▨▨▨ Peak hours only
Jubilee	
Metropolitan	▨▨▨▨▨ Peak hours only
Northern	
Piccadilly	▨▨▨▨▨ Peak hours only
Victoria	
Docklands Light Railway †	▨▨▨▨▨ Under construction
⇌ Network SouthEast	▨▨▨▨▨ Peak hours only

○ Interchange stations
⇌ Connections with British Rail
⊟ Connections within walking distance
✳ Closed Sundays
✳ Closed Saturdays and Sundays
▲ Served by Piccadilly line early mornings and late evenings Monday to Saturday and all day Sundays
◊◊ Closed for reconstruction. Use Edgware Road (Circle/District/H&C) instead
† For opening times see poster journey planners
Certain stations are closed during public holidays

THOMAS & BENACCI LTD
2, Bedale Street
London SE1 - 071-403-2835

© Copyright 1985-1991 by Edizioni Storti - Venice
San Marco, 2551 - Venice Italy
Tel. 41/431607
Fax 41/432347
Printed in Italy

The information in this book is presented in good faith, under
the terms of the Trade Descriptions Act. Every effort has been
made by the publishers to check the facts, but they do not take
responsibility for errors in the information or for changes after
this guide has been printed, for printer's errors etc.

Special thanks to the British Tourist Authority for making the
facilities of their Information Library available to us.

Third Edition revised and up-dated by Peter Matthews
Published by Edizioni Storti s.n.c. Venice-Italy

The Publisher wishes to thank photographers and all the
institutions, museums and galleries listed below for their kind
permission to reproduce photographs in this book.
John Bethell Photography pages: 18, 20/21, 28, 34/35, 45
(below), 48, 49, 51, 52, 53, 54, 55, 62, 64, 65, 66, 67, 68, 69, 71,
72, 73, 75, 76 (above), 83, 88, 90, 93, 95, 97, 99, 102, 103, 107,
110, 117 (below), 119, 120, 124, 125 (below), 128, 132, 134,
137, 142, 145, 146, 148, 149, 154, 159, 160/161, 163, 165, 166/
167, 168, 169, 173, 174, 175, 176, 177, 178, 179, 180/181.
British Tourist Authority pages: 116, 117 (above), 121, 133.
British Crown Copyright page: 155.
Peter Cheze Brown page: 63.
Courtauld Institute Galleries, University of London pages:
129, 130/131.
Camera Press Ltd pages: 24, 25.
Trustees British Museum London pages: 104/105, 108/109,
112, 113.
Trustees National Gallery London pages: 36, 37, 38.
Tate Gallery London pages: 29, 30.
Victoria & Albert Museum London pages: 84, 85, 86.
Eric Rowell pages: 26, 27, 92, 98, 125 (above), 135, 147.